Civil War
RAILROADS
& Models

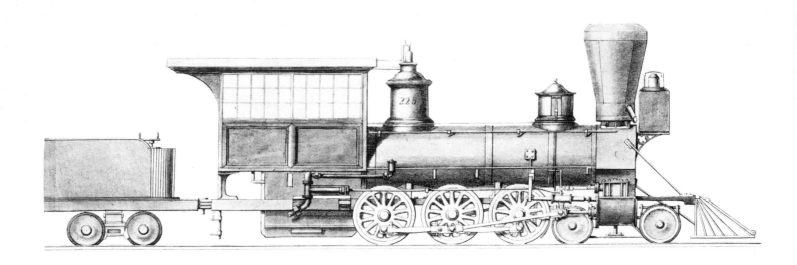

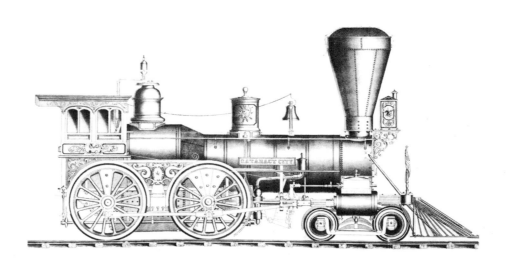

Civil War
RAILROADS
& Models

By Edwin P. Alexander

Clarkson N. Potter, Inc./Publishers NEW YORK
DISTRIBUTED BY CROWN PUBLISHERS, INC.

Published simultaneously in Canada by General Publishing Company Limited.

First edition

Printed in the United States of America

Designed by Katy Homans

Library of Congress Cataloging in Publication Data

Alexander, Edwin P.
    Civil War railroads and models.

    Bibliography: p.
    Includes index.
        1. Railroads—Models. 2. United States—History—
Civil War—Transportation. I. Title.
TF197.A398   1977   625.1′9   77-4680
ISBN 0-517-53073-2

CONTENTS

Picture & Source Credits

Association of American Railroads • *Washington, D.C.*
Baltimore & Ohio Railroad • *Baltimore, Maryland*
Engineering Societies Library • *New York, New York*
Library of Congress • *Washington, D.C.*
Louisville & Nashville Railroad • *Louisville, Kentucky*
National Archives • *Washington, D.C.*
Pennsylvania Railroad • *Philadelphia, Pennsylvania*
Southern Railway • *Washington, D.C.*
U.S. Signal Corps • *Washington, D.C.*

After nearly half a century of collecting railroad material—data, photographs, drawings, etcetera—the actual sources of some of the illustrations are, I regret, impossible to recall. If, therefore, I have overlooked anyone it was not intentional. More recently, some of the contributors have been Graham Claytor, Frank Cornell, Robert Hess, Ward Kimball, Wilbur Kurtz, and Edison Thomas.

Preface

MANY YEARS AGO, in the course of researching general railroad history, I found the subject of Civil War railroads covered in articles, reports, reminiscences, stories of various events, descriptions of famous locomotives, and associated writings. I collected and filed this material with the idea of using it eventually for a book because there was then nothing in print on the subject with the exception of *The Great Locomotive Chase*.

In recent years, however, a number of books on the railroads of the Civil War have appeared, and my concept of how the theme should be treated has changed. Because most of my work has been in building scale models I decided on an approach that would combine historical facts, illustrative material, and data on building scale miniatures of that period. Drawings and information about Civil War railroad equipment have been hard to find, and consequently very little has been built by modelers. It is my hope, then, that this book will stimulate interest in this period for model building.

Because, as the ancient saying so aptly states, "one picture is worth ten thousand words," the illustrative material is an integral part of this book. Eighty percent of the illustrations are from the 1860s, the balance are scale drawings pertaining to miniature construction. Civil War and railroad fans and historians will find that most of the contents are for them, which of course was always my intention. If some readers are persuaded to take up the related hobby of model building, all the better, for they will find it a most rewarding one.

Figure 1. Two field guns of the Boston battery guard the B & O Railroad Relay Bridge.

CHAPTER I
Historical Background

B Y THE 1860s RAILROADS were expanding everywhere. Lines were being extended to open up the then new West, now that the barrier of the Alleghenies had been crossed. Others were reaching out through the South. West of Pittsburgh and north of the Ohio River over ten thousand miles of track had been laid. Approximately the same length of track covered the entire South, and the Northeast, where the population of the country was concentrated, was served by another ten thousand miles of railroad. In the ten years between 1850 and 1860 the country's trackage grew from nine thousand miles to over thirty thousand.

The Civil War had been called the first railroad war because of the important part played by railroads in moving troops and supplies. But in the beginning neither side went into the conflict with any conception of how important the carriers would become. The railroads of the Confederacy not only had half the trackage of those in the Union but they were beset with variations in gauge and a lack of through connections at vital points. North of Richmond the lines were standard gauge (i.e., the modern 4′8½″), whereas south of the city only those to Wilmington, North Carolina, and a few others joining them were standard, everything else being five-foot gauge. Southwest of the Mississippi most of the embryonic roads were five-foot six-inch gauge. An example of the lack of through connections was Richmond itself, with five railroads terminating there but none linked to another, a situation common throughout the South.

In the North by far the most mileage was standard, with the exception being that on the Erie, the Atlantic & Great Western, and the Delaware, Lackawanna & Western, which had six-foot gauge. Through connections in the North were better, more trunk lines had been established, and service was generally better than in the South. The principal bottlenecks were at Baltimore and Washington, and it should be noted that at the outset of the war there were no rail connections between the North and the South, across neither the Potomac nor the Ohio rivers. But with the North's principal cities and seaports well linked by an established rail network, it was far better equipped than the South to provide the rail transportation soon to be demanded by military necessities.

The Northern railroads most affected by the Civil War were the Baltimore & Ohio; Northern Central; Philadelphia, Wilmington & Baltimore; and the Pennsylvania. The Philadelphia, Wilmington & Baltimore was the first railroad to become involved in the conflict, in the spring of 1861, not long after Allan Pinkerton (1819–1884) had arranged

Abraham Lincoln's safe trip to his inaugural over its line. President of the line, Samuel M. Felton, gives details of the plans developed by Pinkerton (this quote, and the ones following in this chapter, are taken verbatim from company reports of the period).

He was a man of great skill and resources, I furnished him with a few hints, and at once set him on the track with eight assistants. There were then drilling upon the line of the railroad some three military organizations, professedly for home defense, pretending to be Union men, and in one or two instances tendering their services to the railroad in case of trouble. Their propositions were duly considered, but the defense of the road was never entrusted to their tender mercies. The first thing done was to enlist a volunteer in each of these military companies. They pretended to come from New Orleans and Mobile and did not appear to be wanting in sympathy for the South. They were furnished with uniforms at the expense of the road, and drilled as often as their associates in arms, became initiated into all the secrets of the organizations, and reported every day or two to their chief who immediately reported to me the designs and plans of these military companies. One of these organizations was loyal, but the other two were disloyal and fully in the plot to destroy the bridges and march to Washington, to wrest it from the hands of the legally constituted authorities. Every nook and corner of the road and its vicinity was explored by the chief and his detectives, and various modes known to and practiced only by detectives were resorted to to win the confidence of the conspirators and get into their secrets. The plan worked well, and the midnight plottings and daily consultations of the conspirators were treasured up as a guide to our future plans for thwarting them. . . . It was made as certain as strong circumstantial and positive evidence could make it that there was a plot to burn the bridges and destroy the road, and murder Mr. Lincoln on his way to Washington if it turned out that he went there before troops were called. If troops were first called, then the bridges were to be destroyed, and Washington cut off and taken possession of by the South. I at once organized and armed a force of about two hundred men whom I distributed along the line between the Susquehanna and Baltimore, principally at the bridges. These men were drilled secretly and regularly by drillmasters, and were apparently employed in whitewashing the bridges, putting on some six or seven coats of whitewash, saturated with salt and alum, to make the outside of the bridges as nearly fireproof as possible. The whitewashing, so extensive in its application, became the nine days' wonder of the neighborhood. Thus the bridges were strongly guarded, and a train was arranged so as to concentrate all the forces at one point in case of trouble.

The careful planning for the protection of the bridges notwithstanding, they were destroyed, thus disabling the road for forty miles south of the Susquehanna River. The secessionists, under the leadership of the notorious Marshal Kane, had been permitted to hold full sway in Baltimore on the nineteenth of April 1861, airing their treason and assailing the troops hastening to the defense of Washington. As night drew on, with an appetite whetted for further action they gleefully decided on a plan of incendiarism. Isaac R. Trimble, a former superintendent of the Philadelphia, Wilmington & Baltimore Railroad Company, was selected by Mayor Brown and Charles Howard, the president of the

Board of Police of Baltimore, to lead a body of men to add to the crime of incendiarism that of treason. Trimble, with 160 men masquerading as policemen and militiamen, assembled about half past three on the morning of the twentieth at the bridge over Harris Creek, within the Baltimore city limits. The bridge was of the Howe truss type, with a 104-foot span and railroad track on one side, a wagon roadway on the other. After firing the bridge Trimble marched his incendiaries to the engine house at Canton, where he awaited the arrival of the night mail. This train, drawn by the engine *America,* with A. O. Denio as engineer, Bowie Rollins as fireman, and Charles Howard as conductor, arrived at 3:14 A.M. and was halted at gunpoint. It was instantly seized by Trimble, who loaded his forces on three cars and started northward, with the intention of scuttling the *Maryland* and burning all the bridges. The train reached Back River Bridge about five o'clock in the morning, where William J. Dealy, a boy telegraph operator who had been stationed there temporarily a few days before, was made prisoner. Then proceeding northward, the train stopped at Magnolia, where James A. Swift, a telegraph operator, was treated in the same manner. The train made no other stops until crossing the Bush River Bridge. When Trimble arrived there, about eight o'clock, and was informed by both Conductor Goodwin and Conductor Howard that a southbound freight train was coming and that troops were concentrating at Perryville, he abandoned the scuttling of the *Maryland.* A large pile of timber just north of the bridge had been stored there for repairs necessary during the year, and was fired. With the fire under way the next move was to fire the draw span, a Howe truss of seventy feet, and wait on the south side of the bridge until the draw was completely destroyed.

This accomplished, the party reembarked and steamed on to Gunpowder Bridge, whose draw, of the same nature and dimensions as the one at Bush River Bridge, was also destroyed. Trimble and his men then made an attempt to destroy the Back River Bridge, but the salt and alum whitewash with which it was covered rendered their efforts futile, so they returned to Canton and marched to the city hall, where they were received in triumph. Trimble claimed that this campaign of incendiarism was ordered by Governor Hicks to prevent troops from passing through Baltimore, but be that as it may, the destruction that marked this plan was accomplished with a fiendish delight, as if in revenge for the company's officers having foiled the plot laid in Baltimore for the assassination of Abraham Lincoln.

The incendiary acts of Trimble and his men disabled the road for forty miles south of the Susquehanna River, but they did not disable it for carrying troops for the defense of the nation's capital. The road was intact from Philadelphia to Perryville, and thus a route was opened via the steamer *Maryland* to Annapolis, then via the Annapolis branch and the Baltimore & Ohio Railroad to Washington. Through this route troops and munitions were carried on the railroad, saving it from capture in a sudden assault. The bridges were repaired and the road opened through to Baltimore on May 14, 1861, without any assistance or protection from the government.

In General Lee's Maryland campaign of 1864, led by Jubal Early against the cities of Baltimore and Washington, Major Harry Gilmor, a Southern partisan ranger, was ordered to cut the Northern Central Railway at or near Cockeysville, and the Philadelphia, Wilmington & Baltimore Railroad between Baltimore and the Susquehanna River. After destroying the bridge over the Gunpowder River on the former, this dashing and intrepid rider took up with 130 men the march for the latter line. He reached Magnolia on the morning of July eleventh and arranged his plans for capturing trains and disabling the road. How well he succeeded is best told in his own words.

We pushed on, and when within a mile and a half of the railroad bridge where the Philadelphia, Wilmington and Baltimore Railroad crosses the Gunpowder, I discovered a passenger train coming on from Baltimore and ordered Captain Bailey, with twenty men, to charge ahead and capture it. The capture was soon effected. Guards were then stationed all around, and I gave strict orders that no plundering should be done, threatening to shoot or cut down the first man I caught in anything of the sort. I also furnished the baggage-master with a guard, telling him to deliver to each passenger their property and to unload the train. The engineer had made his escape, or I should have run up to Havre de Grace and made an effort to burn all the bridges and likewise the larger steamer there.

Finding that I could not run the train up to Havre de Grace I burned it, and prepared to catch that which had left Baltimore forty minutes after this one. I had also sent a flag of truce to the drawbridge, where were 200 infantry and the gunboat "Juniata," sent to protect it, demanding a surrender, and was about ordering some sharpshooters to push them a little, when the second train of twelve passenger cars came up and was easily captured. The engineer of this also escaped, but I took the engine in hand, ran it up to the station, and unloaded in like manner as the first, taking care that each one should have the baggage his checks called for.

While the train was being unloaded I kept a good head of steam upon the engine, and, when everything was clear, ordered Captain Bailey to move up his sharpshooters and try to drive the infantry out on the bridge. He soon reported that they had fled to the gunboat, and setting the train on fire, I backed the whole flaming mass down on the bridge, catching some of the infantry a little way from shore upon the structure, and compelling them to jump into the water. The train was running slowly, and stopped right on the draw, where it burned and fell through, communicating the fire and destroying the most important part of the bridge. The wind was blowing directly toward the gunboat, and she had to drop her anchor and get out of the way. I sent a flag of truce to say I had no objection to her coming to the beach to take passengers to Havre de Grace, which was done.

Major Gilmor's statement requires some correction. The trains he captured were No. 9, known as the Express Mail Passenger, leaving Baltimore at 8:36 A.M., passing Magnolia at 9:25, and arriving at Philadelphia at 12:48 P.M., and No. 10, the Morning Mail Passenger, leaving Baltimore at 10:21, passing Magnolia at 11:15 and arriving at Philadelphia at 3:00 P.M. On the morning in question No. 9 was conducted by John Monshower, No. 10 by Thomas Brison. After looting No. 9 Gilmor set fire to its engine cab, destroying about half of it, but none of the cars were burned. After No. 10 was stopped and the mail and baggage removed, it was set afire and started southward. When the burning train reached Gunpowder Bridge it was moving very slowly and was boarded by some Union soldiers, who stopped it on the bridge about 350 feet from the north end. The burning cars set fire to the bridge, which was burned the length of the train, causing the engine to drop into the river. If Captain Bailey was ordered by Gilmor to the bridge to drive the Union forces away he never materialized at that point. A company of the Fourth New York Infantry held the north end of the bridge and, supported by the gunboat *Juniata*, were not assailed. Gilmor remained at Magnolia only a short time after looting the train before taking a hurried departure.

General Lee was reported to have said, "The cutting of the Philadelphia Road was the

only part of the programme in the Maryland campaign that was carried out successfully."
The Northern Central was affected even earlier in the war.

> The road being close to the line dividing the contending parties, was an object
> of attack during the whole war period. . . . On the 20th of April, 1861, an armed
> party, under the direction and Police Commissioners of Baltimore, sallied forth
> from that city and destroyed bridges and other property on the road, entailing a
> damage of $117,609.93. At the same time another armed force of the state of
> Maryland took possession of the Calvert Street Station and General Offices and
> stationed sentinels there, so that neither ingress nor egress could be had without
> making known the countersign. It was on account of this action that the authorities
> temporarily removed the General Offices to Harrisburg.
>
> During the Gettysburg campaign Lee's army destroyed all bridges between
> Hanover Junction and Goldsboro, twelve in number, and nineteen on the
> Wrightsville Branch, all crippled cars at York, and crippled and other cars on
> sidings at Gettysburg, entailing a direct loss of $110,400.

Joseph N. DuBarry, a young superintendent in charge of the Northern Central,
played a part in an anecdote that indicates his concern.

> One instance of his [DuBarry's] stirring zeal was in connection with the
> movement of the train containing ammunition to be hurried forward to
> Hagerstown so as to enable the renewal of the battle of Antietam by McClellan.
> Called from his bed at midnight, he stationed himself in the telegraph office at
> Harrisburg and called into consultation Mr. Samuel S. Blair at Baltimore, whose
> practical knowledge of railroading was invaluable in the crisis, as it was during the
> whole war period, and has been ever since. They both remained on duty through-
> out the night, clearing the tracks and arranging for a through run. As the night
> wore away, Mr. DuBarry's impatience at the delay south of Baltimore, and which
> was beyond his control, knew no bounds; but when the belated train reached him
> at 7:27 A.M. of September 18, 1862, he did not lose a second of time in hurrying it
> on its way, and actually delivered it to the Cumberland Valley Railroad at
> Bridgeport at 10:20 A.M. making the run of eighty-four miles in two hours and
> fifty-three minutes. When it is considered that the train was composed of four
> Baltimore and Ohio freight cars, controlled by hand brakes, with none of the more
> modern appliances, their journal boxes smoking most of the distance, and run-
> ning over a road imperfectly ballasted, iron and aligned, it will readily be seen how
> remarkable was the run, a run never tried before nor equalled since, and the
> unusual nerve of the man that directed it.

The third of the Pennsylvania Railroad affiliated roads involved was the Cumberland
Valley Railroad. The report continues:

> Located as it is both north and south of Mason and Dixon's Line, it [the
> road] suffered very severely during the Civil War. During the years 1861–65
> every mile of it, with the exception of the short distance between Whitehill and the
> Susquehanna, had been visited by Southern troops. Twice the Army of Northern

Virginia visited it, and several times predatory bands committed depredations upon it and the country bordering it. In September 1862, the invasion of Maryland penetrated to the Pennsylvania State line, and all business other than the transportation of troops and munitions of war suspended on the road for several weeks. In October of that year a cavalry raid around the army of the Potomac penetrated as far as Chambersburg. There the Confederates seized and burned Cumberland Valley Railroad property, consisting of wood shop, machine shop, blacksmith shop, engine house, wood sheds and passenger depot, with contents. Three second-class engines were partially destroyed, but afterwards rebuilt. They were the "Utility," "Pioneer," and "Jenny Lind" of Seth Wilmarth's make. In the Gettysburg campaign in 1863 the advance of General Lee's army entered Chambersburg on June 15th, and the railroad was practically in the hands of the enemy for a month. The advance under General Jenkins reached Oyster's Point near the Susquehanna. On that campaign General Lee's forces destroyed the engine house at Hagerstown, the machine and wood shops and the engine house which had been erected in place of the ones destroyed the year before at Chambersburg, as well as the railroad for five miles on each side of that town, the water station at Greencastle, and the Carlisle and Scotland bridges. Again, in July 1864, when Chambersburg was burned, whatever property had been temporarily erected was destroyed. On this last raid all the machinery was saved and kept on cars throughout July and August. The direct losses by these several attacks was not less than $125,000, while the indirect loss by interruption to business was far greater.

The road was strained at times to keep up with governmental requisitions but it never failed to meet them. Its achievement in the movement of the special ammunition train rushing to the aid of McClellan on Antietam's gory field is worthy of record. That train, consisting of four Baltimore and Ohio Railroad Company's cars, in the custody of Lieutenant Bradford of the Ordnance Department, United States Army, was delivered to the Cumberland Valley Railroad by the Northern Central Railway Company at Bridgeport at 10:20 A.M. Thursday, September 18th, 1862. The train was detained at Bridgeport twenty-four minutes, taking on an additional car of ammunition which had been loaded at Harrisburg from the Pennsylvania State Arsenal, and in cooling off the journal boxes of the four cars. It was then made up by attaching to it the locomotive "Judge Watts" under the charge of Joseph Miller as engineer and conductor, and dispatched at 10:44 A.M. It arrived at Chambersburg at 12 M. and at Hagerstown at 12:42 P.M., making the run over the Cumberland Valley Railroad, a distance of seventy-four miles, in one hour and fifty-eight minutes, or an average of one mile in one minute thirty and six-sevenths seconds, an equivalent of over thirty-seven miles an hour. The running time was faster than this, for ten minutes was lost at both Newville and Chambersburg in cooling off the boxes. Deducting the stops, the speed of the train reached forty-five miles per hour. Such running was never experienced on the Cumberland Valley Railroad before, and has not been equaled since. When the train entered Hagerstown all the journal boxes on the four Baltimore and Ohio cars were ablaze.

The actual running time from Baltimore to Hagerstown, a distance of 158 miles, was four hours and thirty-one minutes, or thirty-six and nine-tenths miles

Figure 2. Another view of the Relay Bridge.

per hour. Perhaps there is not another instance in the history of the world where ammunition has been moved such a distance with so much rapidity, and in the face of smoking and blazing journal boxes on the vehicles carrying it.

The railroad that incurred the most damage and interference to traffic in the East, as well as having a number of its locomotives stolen, was the Baltimore & Ohio. The following chronicle from the official reports dated 1861 to 1863 graphically indicates the B & O's vulnerability and the destruction it suffered.

On the night of 18th April, 1861, a detachment of United States regulars, guarding the arsenal at Harper's Ferry, after setting fire to the buildings, evacuated that point. At 10 P.M. Virginia State troops, from Winchester and Charlestown, marched in and took possession, placing a guard of infantry and artillery upon our bridge and from that time throughout the year losses by fire and flood were frequent. The trains continued to run, with many interruptions, until May 25th, 1861, at which time the large rock supported by masonry, near the Point of Rocks, sixty-nine miles from Baltimore, was undermined and thrown upon the track. On the day following, Buffalo Creek bridges Nos. 2 and 3, three hundred and fourteen miles from Baltimore were burned. These bridges consisted of five spans of fifty-two and fifty-four feet each, of iron superstructure, with wooden chord. They were trestled in two days, and in one month restored to their former condition.

This destruction was the precursor of losses which followed in rapid succession. They will be noted chronologically.

1861

May 24th   Telegraph line destroyed near Grafton.

May 28th   Patterson's Creek bridge, two spans, 72 feet 6 inches each, 170 miles from Baltimore; also pump house and Engine adjoining, and Canal span, North Branch Bridge, one span 131 feet, 172 miles from Baltimore, were burned. These were covered wooden bridges, and were in excellent condition.

June 2nd   Opequan Bridge, one span, 147 feet 8 inches, 56 feet high, 97 miles from Baltimore, destroyed, and more than fifty loaded coal cars run into the chasm. These continued to burn for two months, and so intense was the heat that wheels and axles were melted.

June 13th   Pillar Bridge at Martinsburg, 9 spans, 40 feet each, destroyed, and one engine and a number of cars run into it. Also two small bridges burned.

June 14th   Harper's Ferry covered wooden bridge, 7 spans, one of 122 feet, one of 76, four of 127, and one of 131 feet in length. Also flooring, rail-joist, cross ties, double track and iron hand railing of 70 spans, 15 feet each, on iron trestling, through arsenal yard, destroyed.

June 13th   Great Cacapon, two spans, 132 feet 6 inches each, 132 miles from Baltimore, burned.

June 18th   Little Cacapon Bridge, one span, 131 feet, 157 miles from Baltimore, burned.

June 20th   Tuscarora Bridge, 1 span, 39 feet 6 inches, 99 miles from Baltimore, burned.

June 20th   Winchester iron span, at Harper's Ferry, (wood work) burned, and engine 165 run through bridge into Potomac River.

June & July   Engines and cars burned at Martinsburg, and engine, rigger's car and two gondolas burned at Piedmont.

June 25th   Cherry Run iron bridges, two of 25 feet span, 113 miles from Baltimore, thrown off the abutments, and one Camp car, one Derrick car and five Ballast cars burned.

June 27th   Back Creek. The magnificent and costly stone arch, 80 feet span, 110 miles from Baltimore, blown up.

July 21st   The trestling of 21st section bridge was commenced, and on the 25th trains run through from Wheeling to Cumberland.

July   Water station at Martinsburg destroyed.

August   The trestling of Potomac at Harper's Ferry was commenced, but progressed with difficulty, owing to the high stage of water. The work was stopped on the 19th on account of withdrawal of the United States forces from vicinity.

Aug. & Sept. Thirty-six and a half miles of track torn up between Harper's Ferry and Paxton's Cut, and the iron and several thousand ties and track fixtures were transported by animal power to Southern roads.

Sept. 27th Telegraph Line between Adamstown and Point of Rocks destroyed. Five trestles washed out 21st section bridge.

Sept. 29th All the trestling of Potomac River at Harper's Ferry, erected up to August 19, 1861, was carried away by a freshet, with the exception of two trestles adjoining Maryland shore.

Oct. 3rd These were replaced and trains crossed over.

Oct. 8th Rail joist and cross-ties on E span, South Branch iron bridge burned by Confederate forces.

Oct. 23rd Water station, engine house and pumping engine, at Little Cacapon burned. Also two water stations at No. 12, and the pump house, pumping engine, wood house, sand house and blacksmith shop.

Nov. 2nd A portion of the Potomac River, or 21st Section, trestling swept out by freshet and five flat cars, with which it was weighted, carried down the river. The drift wood was within three feet of the track, and the water higher than at any previous period.

Nov. 2nd The George's Creek road was greatly damaged by a freshet, and a number of Baltimore and Ohio iron hopper cars, weighing 41 tons each, were carried by the current down the stream, some of them a distance of two miles. These cars were sent up this road for safety at the time of the raid upon Piedmont.

Nov. 2nd This freshet also carried away the platforms at Sir John's Run.

Nov. 6th Commenced restoring the trestling on 21st Section; the passenger trains between Cumberland and Wheeling continued to run regularly by transferring passengers and baggage at this point.

Nov. 10th All trains crossed over, and business west of Cumberland fully resumed. Commenced removing debris of canal span of bridge over North Branch of the Potomac, six miles east of Cumberland. Since the burning of this bridge, in May 1861, it had not been in the power of the Company to effect repairs east of Cumberland.

Nov. 12th Completed trestling of canal span, North Branch Bridge, and restored wood work and track upon the three iron spans.

Nov. 14th Completed Patterson's Creek trestling, 8 miles east of Cumberland, and military trains ran to Green Spring, 16 miles east of Cumberland.

Nov. 25th The two water stations, blacksmith shop, sand houses and coal bins at Sir John's Run, burned.

Nov. 26th Commenced restoring wood work on east span, South Branch iron bridge.

Figure 3. From a lithograph of the early 1850s, the covered B & O bridge at Harper's Ferry seen from the east bank, before the 1852 Bollman span.

Nov. 27th   Finished South Branch Bridge.

Nov. 30th   Sent an engine and train, with lumber, to Little Cacapon.

Dec. 1st   Finished trestling Little Cacapon.

Dec. 11th   Moving eastward as rapidly as military protection is afforded. Six months had elapsed since a car had passed Little Cacapon. The track was covered in many places by washes from the hill-sides; also, obstructed by rocks and trees; the train went as far as Great Cacapon, 46 miles east of Cumberland. The unexpected appearance of a locomotive and train was hailed with demonstrations of joy by the inhabitants along the road.

Dec. 12th   Commenced trestling Great Cacapon.

Dec. 16th   Finished the trestling, and trains ran to Hancock.

December   During this month trestled Potomac River at Piedmont; also, put George's Creek road in such order as to get the engines and cars from it. The destruction of tracks between Harper's Ferry and Back Creek, removal of rails, cross-ties, track fixtures, etc. continued; four miles were removed after date of last Chronological table, making a total of 40 miles, 2,261 feet of track torn up, and the iron for nearly thirty-seven miles taken away. The destruction of the telegraph line and removal of the wires also continued.

1862

Jan. 2nd   Water station at North Mountain burned.

Jan. 4th   Passenger train from Hancock arrived in Cumberland on time, but did not return on account of fighting at Bath, near Sir John's Run.

Jan. 5th   Attack on Hancock; no trains running east of Green Spring. Great Cacapon trestling burned; also two houses adjacent, belonging to the Company.

Jan. 8th   A train went to Great Cacapon.

Jan. 11th   No trains running east of Patterson's Creek.

Jan. 31st   Running to Patterson's Creek, and military train to South Branch since 11th January. United States troops burned six pens for loading cattle at Patterson's Creek, and used the Railroad, between Patterson's Creek and North Branch as a wagon road.

Feb. 7th   United States forces, under Col. Geary crossed over into Harper's Ferry and burned the Company's Hotel, warehouse, ticket office and water station; also, 38 panels, 570 feet in length, of wood work on the double track iron trestling through Arsenal yard and boatway bridge. This was the remainder of the Company's property in Harper's Ferry, not destroyed by the enemy. These troops also destroyed the blacksmith shop at Calico Rock, and the skiffs and flatboats built for use in trestling.

Feb. 8th   Inspection train went as far east as Great Cacapon Bridge, the trestling of which was found to be badly burned and cut.

Feb. 11th   Commenced retrestling Great Cacapon. Finished it on the 14th. This opened the road eastward to Hancock.

Feb. 13th   Meyer's water station burned.

Feb. 26th   Guards taken from Patterson's Creek, and at night the rail joist on trestling over said stream was burned, and the track destroyed, cutting off communication between Gen. Lander's forces at Paw Paw and Cumberland. Repaired and trains crossed over on 27th.

March 1st   Commenced trestling Sleepy Creek; weather very severe; snow, rain, sleet and ice. Finished it on 5th; also, repaired the bridge at Cherry Run.

March 4th   Orders given for vigorous prosecution of the work at reopening from each end of burnt district. The forces working eastward, under W. E. Porter, Assistant Master of Road, came to Back Creek on 5th inst. This bridge was originally a stone arch of eighty feet span. The opening made by its destruction was 130 feet in length and 67 feet deep. A temporary wire suspension bridge was at once thrown across the chasm, and over this the iron and cross-ties were carried, and the work at track laying commenced. At the same time the bridge forces, under W. Allee, Supervisor of Bridges, commenced clearing the ruins, preparatory to the erection of the heavy and difficult work of trestling, and crossed trains over it on 10th of said month, at 3 P.M., when the track laying was pressed rapidly by the forces under Geo. W. Cromwell, Wm. R. Mudge, John M. Harman, Bryan Healey, John B. Stewart and Jas. Dawson, Supervisors of Track, and W. Zumbro, Supervisor of Water Stations; reaching Martinsburg on 14th. Another force, under W. C. Quiney, then Acting Master of Road, with Thos. Heskett, Supervisor of Bridges, and W. M. Shawen, J. P. Williams, C. H. Mayers and Geo. Henthorn, Supervisors of Track, and Benjamin Uncles, Supervisor of Water Stations— repaired to Harper's Ferry on the 4th, to commence working westward. Owing to the great depth of water and the swiftness of the current, it was found impossible to raise the trestles in the Potomac River. A dangerous and difficult task was performed. Large cables were stretched across the river, by means of which the heavy timbers to restore the line of wood work 1620 feet in length upon the original iron trestling through the arsenal yard in Harper's Ferry, and to trestle the Tilt Hammer Bridge, also the iron rails, track fixtures and cross-ties, were rafted over the river and hoisted to their position. Frequent efforts were made by lashing boats to the cables and to the masonry, to raise trestles in the river. On the 5th, one was placed in position, but in consequence of the excessive cold, the ropes becoming stiffened by ice, the force was again sent to the work through arsenal yard, and upon the Tilt Hammer Bridge. This bridge was completed on the 6th. On the 9th, the forces were put upon four of the river spans, but their most energetic efforts were unequal to the power of the elements. On the 10th, heavy rain all day, but trestling in river progressed. From the rain of the 10th, the river continued too full, and the current too swift, to accomplish much at the main bridge on the 11th.

March 12th   On the 12th, work was resumed on the main bridge, and pressed with all possible energy until the night of the 18th, when the first locomotive, for nine months, went over into Harper's Ferry.

March 19th   On the 19th, the track was completed on iron trestling through Arsenal Yard. All this work in Harper's Ferry, including the Tilt Hammer Bridge, would have been done in much less time if the main bridge could have been completed first; but the time saved fully repaid all the disadvantages in getting the materials for it across the river, and for the additional labor required to accomplish the work.

March 20th   On the 20th, track laying was commenced near the 83rd mile post, and progressed rapidly. The track was joined and the road reopened on the 29th March. As an evidence that all this work was carefully performed, although with so much rapidity, on the 30th nearly eight hundred cars passed safely over it. The water stations at Harper's Ferry, Martinsburg, North Mountain, Sir John's Run, No. 12, Little Cacapon and Patterson's Creek were rebuilt, and water in abundance provided. The telegraph line was fully restored, and sufficient side tracks for facilitating the movement of trains were laid, and all the arrangements for prompt working were complete, and the road ready for the immense business at once thrown upon it. The burnt engines at Duffields, and those at Martinsburg, as also portions of the burnt cars, were sent to the different shops for repairs.

Figure 4. A Confederate battery overlooking Harper's Ferry and bridge, June 1861. The bridge was destroyed June 14.

April 9th High water and seven inches of snow, with heavy accumulations of drift against all the bridge trestling on the line, requiring great exertions to save it. Two trestles were washed out at Patterson's Creek. Repaired on the 10th and trains passed over.

April 13-16 Water again very high. It was necessary to stand loaded cars upon the Potomac trestling at Harper's Ferry, to weigh it down.

April 22nd River again very high, and cars put upon trestling at Back Creek, Opequan, Sleepy Creek, Great Cacapon and Patterson's Creek, to keep water from raising them from their foundation. At 11:30 A.M. the curved span of Harper's Ferry trestling, adjoining the Maryland shore, and two contiguous spans, were swept out, and fourteen loaded coal cars went into the river. At 3:15 P.M. a canal boat having floated over the tow path came against the next span and swept it out with ten loaded cars, and at 7:45 P.M. one-half of the wide span with 12 cars went out. The water continued at such great height that trestling could not be commenced until April 28th. Passengers and baggage were transferred by boats.

May 4th On the 4th day of May it was finished, and 400 loaded cars passed over it.

May 18th Commenced relaying 2nd track from Martinsburg westward.

Figure 5.   Harper's Ferry after destruction of the arsenal, end of May 1861.

May 25th   Federal forces retreated from Winchester through Martinsburg. The Company's employees also left this vicinity.

May 28th   Opequan, Pillar and Back Creek trestling burned.

June 2nd   Trestling at Great Cacapon damaged by high water, but repaired in a few hours.

June 2-3   Forces repaired to Opequan and Back Creek.

June 4th   Back Creek trestling repaired, and force from there moved to Pillar Bridge, but on account of heavy rains they were sent Westward to save other trestling between Martinsburg and Cumberland, and the force from Opequan sent to Harper's Ferry to keep drift clear.

June 5th   Great Cacapon trestling , and one trestle in Little Cacapon, carried away by a freshet; also four-and-a-half spans at Harper's Ferry. Back Creek also damaged.

June 6th   Back Creek, Little Cacapon and Opequan repaired.

June 7th   Remainder of Potomac River trestling at Harper's Ferry, from shore to shore carried out by high water.

June 8th   Great Cacapon retrestled; also Pillar Bridge at Martinsburg finished. Road again open from Harper's Ferry to Wheeling. Through passenger trains ran regularly. The passengers and baggage transferred by boats. Stock trains were also run, the stock being likewise transferred by boats.

June 9th   Forces from east and west commenced retrestling Potomac River at Harper's Ferry, and completed it on the 15th.

June 22nd   Resumed work on 2nd track west of Martinsburg, and completed it to Paxton's Cut July 9th.

July 17th   Constructed track from top of bank to water in Opequan to recover the wrecked cars. They were all taken out during the month.

July 24th   Commenced raising iron bridge at Harper's Ferry with No. 4 span. In consequence of the frequent delays at this point by trestling washing out, it was determined to risk the iron bridge.

August 21st   United States troops left Berlin, cut 26 telegraph poles and destroyed the wire. Two iron spans, Nos. 3 and 4 of the magnificent bridge at Harper's Ferry completed during the month, and preparations made to erect span No. 5. The cars lost in the river at the time the trestling was swept away, were also taken out during this month and sent to Baltimore and Piedmont for repairs.

Sept. 6th   United States forces retreated from Martinsburg.

Sept. 8th   The splendid iron suspension bridge at Monocacy blown up by the enemy. This bridge consisted of three spans of 115 feet each. The water station at Monocacy, including pump house and engine, also burned.

Sept. 13th   Pillar Bridge at Martinsburg again destroyed.

Sept. 15th   Commenced removing debris of Monocacy bridge. This vicinity was the camping ground of the Confederate army, and before operations could be commenced at the bridge, dead men, horses and cattle had to be buried.

Sept. 16th   Opequan trestling again destroyed.

Sept. 17th   Government Canal Bridge at Harper's Ferry destroyed. This was a covered wooden bridge, 148 feet span, and the only one between Monocacy and Cumberland that remained intact up to this period. Monocacy trestling commenced; crossed trains over at 11 A.M., September 21.

Sept. 22nd   Back Creek trestling destroyed.

Sept. 24th   Reconstruction train went to Harper's Ferry. The iron spans Nos. 3 and 4, also Winchester iron span, blown up and laying in confused masses in the river. The trestling in other spans all destroyed, also 24 spans of wood work on iron trestling, Boatway bridge, Wasteway 12 spans, two bridges of 13½ spans at Beck's Quarry, and carpenter shop at Harper's Ferry, tool house and blacksmith shop, burned. Also ten house cars burned in Harper's Ferry, and 14 in Quarry siding, 3 gondola cars run into the river, 4 house and 2 crane cars thrown into the Chesapeake and Ohio Canal. Engine No. 30 burned and hanging in trestlework at west end of bridge, and engine No. 166 burned in Harper's Ferry tunnel. Information of great destruction to road and Company's property at Martinsburg.

Sept. 25th   Workmen commenced removal of wrecks of cars, engines and iron bridge at Harper's Ferry; also restoring damage to iron trestling, Boatway Bridge, Wasteway; also retrestling the Main and Government Canal Bridge. The water station at Monocacy was rebuilt during the month. The transfer of coal from canal boats into B. & O. cars at Sandy Hook continued from close of last fiscal year. Additional derricks were erected, and by this means the supply of coal for Company's use east of Harper's Ferry, and upon the Washington Branch, was fully maintained. Large quantities of gas coal from Newburg were also transferred. 14,425 cross-ties, and the lumber for relaying the Howard Street track, were also brought from the Western portion of the road via canal from Cumberland to Sandy Hook.

In the western theatre of war, the Louisville & Nashville Railroad was seriously affected during the years 1861 to 1865. The following excerpts, for the year ending June 30, 1862, are from the annual reports of Albert Fink, Engineer and Superintendent of the Machinery and Road Department, and indicate some of the extensive damage sustained.

On the 4th of July, 1861, the authorities of the State of Tennessee seized the trains on the Tennessee part of the road, and from that time until February last, that part of the road was therefore not operated by the Company. . . . Part of this property came again into the hands of the Company last February, after the Southern forces had left the line of the road. . . . On the 17th of September, 1861, the forces of the Southern Confederacy took possession of the southern part of the road, and came up as far as the Rolling Fork River, and burned the bridge over that stream. The only part of the road which at that time could be operated by the Company, was from Louisville to Rolling Fork, 30 miles, and from Lebanon Junction to Lebanon, 37 miles, making a total of 67 miles.

On the 18th of September, the Federal forces advanced to the Rolling Fork bridge. This bridge consisted of two spans 200 feet each, crossing the river at an elevation of 65 feet. The erection of a temporary trestle work was commenced on the 20th, and trains passed over it on the 2nd of October.

After Rolling Fork Bridge was repaired, during which time the Federal forces had advanced to Green River, Bacon Creek bridge was rebuilt a second time, and completed on the 12th of December.

The bridge over Green River is 1,000 feet long and consists of five spans of iron superstructure, crossing the river at an elevation of 115 feet. In anticipation of an advance of the Federal forces in October, which did not take place before the middle of December, the Confederate forces had destroyed two southern spans of the bridge, by blowing up the southern pier, which was 90 feet high. The second pier from the south, had been mined and an attempt made to blow it up too, but fortunately it did not succeed. The two spans which were destroyed are, in the ordinary stage of the river, over dry land, and a trestle can be kept up there without any danger of its being reached by current or driftwood, even in high stages of water.

The clearing away of the wreck was commenced on the 17th of December, and the trestle work, 390 feet long and 100 feet high at the highest place, was ready for the passage of trains on the 8th of January.

The Federal forces did not advance beyond Green River until the 12th of February, when they commenced to march towards Bowling Green and Nashville, and the road south of Green River passed again into the hands of the Company. The condition of the road below Green River was as follows: The depots at Rowlett's, Horse Cave, Woodland, Cave City, Glasgow Junction, Rocky Hill, Oakland, Bowling Green, and Woodburn, were burned. Also, the machine shop and engine house at Bowling Green, and the water station at Prewitt's Knob. The track was destroyed between mile 77 and 81, in ten different places by piling cord wood on the track, setting it on fire, thus burning the cross-ties, and bending the rails. Between mile 81 and 87, the track was not injured, but between mile 87 and 91, three and three quarter miles of track had been torn up, the cross-ties burned and the rails bent. On the last day of February, the track was repaired and the road in running order to Barren River.

The day before the Federal forces reached Barren River, the bridge over that stream, consisting of two spans of iron superstructure, crossing at an elevation of 60 feet, was entirely destroyed by blowing up the stone pillars on which the superstructure rested. The continuation of high water in Barren River, made it impossible to commence as early as was desirable the construction of a temporary bridge. The first trestle was raised on the 14th of March, when the work was again interrupted for a week by a freshet thus delaying its completion until the 8th of April. The trestle work had to be built on a sharp curve, so as to avoid the wreck of the iron bridge, which could not be removed during the high stage of water. . . .

On the road south of Bowling Green was found a part of the rolling stock of the Company, and some cars of southern roads, which were left in the hurry of the retreat. Cars and engines were in a dilapidated condition. Wrecks, which had accumulated during the administration of the road under the Southern Confederacy, were strewn along the road at all points. Of the sixteen engines taken from us, ten were recovered. Five of these were at the time undergoing repairs at the Bowling Green shops, and were in the fire when the Engine House and Machine Shop were burned, but were not materially injured. One of the engines was on the south side of the Cumberland River, one was lying in the Cumberland River, having been run off from the draw bridge, a third one was wrecked on the road, leaving only two available for service. They were made use of to run a daily train between Bowling Green and Edgefield, opposite Nashville, before Barren River bridge was completed, and the rolling stock of the northern end could be brought into service. The track between Bowling Green and Nashville was found in a very bad condition. Little or no work had been done on it during the administration of the road under the Southern Confederacy. On the 15th of March the train ran off the track ten miles north of Nashville; and when the only remaining engine south of Bowling Green was sent with workmen to remove the wreck, it was captured by Morgan, who suddenly made his appearance at Gallatin, twenty-six miles in the rear of the Federal army, which was then at, and south of Nashville. Morgan damaged the engine, burned thirteen cars on the Gallatin siding, and burned the water house, and wood sawing and pumping machinery. This put a stop to the operation of the road between Bowling Green and Edgefield, until one of the engines belonging to the United States Government, and intended for the operation of the roads south of Nashville was placed on our road, and the daily train resumed between Bowling Green and Edgefield, until the completion of the Barren River bridge, on the 8th of April, when, for the first time since July 4th, 1861, the trains ran through from Louisville to Edgefield. . . .

On the 11th of May, Morgan again appeared with a small force at Cave City, 100 miles north of Nashville, and captured a freight and passenger train, destroying thirty-seven freight cars (twenty-seven of which belonged to the Company) and three passenger cars. Since that time, up to July 1st, no further damage has been done to the road by Confederate forces. . . .

The loss in rolling stock sustained during the year, has been:

6 Locomotives lost, and 10 damaged
14 Passenger Cars lost
3 Baggage Cars lost
142 Box Cars
30 Flat Cars lost

The estimate of damage done . . . is $386,971.04. . . .

During the twelve months, from July 1, 1862 to July 1, 1863, the Road has only been operated for its entire length for seven months and twelve days. The Main Stem, from Edgefield, opposite Nashville, and the Memphis, Lebanon and Bardstown Branches, were at various times during the year in the possession of the Confederate forces, with the exception of some twenty miles north and twenty miles south of Bowling Green. For a period of two weeks trains could not even venture to leave Louisville. . . .

The first raid made by Morgan took place about the middle of July, 1862. After threatening Bowling Green and Munfordville, he suddenly made his appearance at Lebanon where he captured the Federal forces and destroyed the Government stores, without however materially damaging the railroad. One month later, on the 12th of August, Morgan took possession of Gallatin, captured the Federal forces stationed there, destroyed a train of twenty-nine cars, the water station, a bridge two and a half miles south, and another six miles north of Gallatin. He also captured the Federal forces on Tunnel Hill, seven miles north of Gallatin and set the timber-work on fire, which supported the roof and sides of the tunnel.

It was supposed, that after having thus effectually interrupted the communication between Louisville and Nashville, Morgan would again leave the line of the Road; but, when, on the following day, without waiting for military protection, a force of our workmen were sent to Gallatin, to repair the track, squads of Confederates made their appearance and drove them off. On the 14th, a force of our Bridge Carpenters was sent from Bowling Green, by way of the Nashville and Kentucky Railroad, to the bridge two and a half miles south of Gallatin. A guard was sent with them by the Commander of the post of Nashville. The party had been but one day at the bridge, when they were attacked by the Confederates, who were still in the neighborhood in force. At first the Confederates were driven off, but they were reinforced and our troops fell back towards Nashville. (During this fight one of our workmen was killed). The Confederates pursued our troops, capturing the bridge guards and destroying the bridges on their route, until they reached Dry Creek Bridge, nine miles from Nashville, where they were at last arrested, through the gallant resistance made by the guard stationed there. . . .

A large Confederate army under General Kirby Smith had entered Central Kentucky, and having defeated the Federal troops about the 1st of September, at Richmond, Lexington fell into their hands, whence they threatened Cincinnati and Louisville. Numerous squads of cavalry were sent out by them to make raids on our Road, and on the 7th of September, the newly built Salt River Bridge, at Shepherdsville, eighteen miles from Louisville, was partially destroyed by a force of Confederates, after they had captured the guard stationed there. On the 10th of September the bridge over Rolling Fork, at New Haven, on the Lebanon Branch, met with the same fate. This work of destruction being done by small forces, who retreated as soon as they had accomplished their object, we were enabled to commence rebuilding Salt River Bridge on the 8th of September. Trains passed over it again on the 13th of September, but they were not the regular trains to resume the business of the Road, they were fugitive trains going north to escape Bragg's forces, which were rapidly advancing into Kentucky, having reached already Cave City, on the 12th, and were then marching on Munfordville. The only train that passed over Salt River Bridge, going south, after the bridge had been rebuilt, and before it was again destroyed, was the train sent by General Boyle, on the night of the 13th and 14th of September, with reinforcements for the garrison, in the fortifications of Green River Bridge. Six miles from its destination this train was thrown from the track, at a place where the Road had been undermined by Bragg's advance guards, and all the cars were destroyed during that day. The reinforcements, however, reached the fortification at Green River by a circuitous route, in time to take part in the fight, which took place the same day, and which resulted in the repulse of the Confederates. On the 16th, Bragg renewed the attack with increased numbers, and compelled the garrison to surrender on the 17th. Green River Bridge was burned, and the whole Road to Louisville laid now at the mercy of the invading enemy. . . .

On the 18th of September, when it was ascertained that Bragg's army was rapidly advancing on Louisville, no more trains left this place. The work at the Company's shops was suspended, and the workmen and employees organized into military companies, in order to be prepared with the other citizens for the defense of Louisville. Up to the 23rd it appeared doubtful whether Bragg's or Buell's forces would reach here first. On the 25th, Buell's army began to arrive in the city; Bragg with his main forces having come to a halt near Bardstown. . . .

(25th of November—after much reconstruction) The many trains that were all at once put on the Road, made it necessary to employ a great many new men, who were unacquainted with the Road, and whose capacities could often only be ascertained by actual trial. The want of a sufficient track force on the road that had not been worked for several months, and which could not even be properly examined before it was thrown open for business caused the trains to run off in several instances. The want of wood and water at the proper places also interfered with the regularity of the trains. The wood train, having no right to the Road when other trains were not on time, could not supply the deficiency. Five or six trains would sometimes arrive at a water station, which was built to supply two only, and at other times a sudden frost would disable all the pumps, when no water at all could be obtained.

However, as soon as the Road was re-opened to Nashville, all the available rolling stock of the Company, together with the Government cars and engines, taken from the roads south of Nashville, was put on the Road, with a view to do all the business the Army of the Cumberland might require, but without proper regard to the condition or capacity of the Road. Under the existing circumstances, it could hardly be expected that everything should work smoothly. The numerous causes of delay and interruption, sometimes acting singly, often together—could not be removed in one day; and the fact that the Road performed the work it actually did, is due to the untiring energy and faithfulness of the employees, and should have been the subject to praise rather than complaint.

Nevertheless, complaints were made by the military authorities, and intimation was given that the management of the Road would be taken out of the hands of the Company and handed over to the military officers. It seemed to be taken for granted, that because the Road could not carry as much freight as the Army of the Cumberland then chanced to require, it must necessarily be badly managed. Had not better councils prevailed, it would soon have been apparent that, to the numerous unavoidable difficulties, many others that were unavoidable would have been added without remedying any. . . .

On the 25th of December [1862] exactly one month after the Road had been reopened to Nashville, General Morgan made his appearance at Glasgow with from 3,000 to 4,000 men. Thence he moved north, parallel with the Road, and, avoiding the fortifications at Munfordville, struck our Road at Bacon Creek, eight miles north of that place. From that place he swept over the Road for a distance of thirty-five miles, burning and destroying all bridges, culverts, depots, water stations, fire wood, etc. on his route. On the 27th he had reached Elizabethtown, which place he bombarded, forcing the Federal force stationed there to surrender. On the 28th, he attacked the fortifications on Muldraugh's Hill, where the garrison also surrendered, giving Morgan possession of the heavy trestle-works, which he immediately reduced to a heap of ashes. His advance guards came within twenty-eight miles of Louisville, where they burned Cane Run bridge. Two bridges on the Lebanon Branch, but recently permanently reconstructed, were also burned, and preparations had been made to destroy every important structure on that part of the Road when, fortunately, Colonel Harlan, who had been sent by General Rosecrans in pursuit of Morgan caught up with him on the 30th, at Rolling Fork, and arrested his further movements north. Morgan left the line of the Road, after having destroyed 2,290 feet of bridging, besides three depots, three water stations, and a number of culverts and cattle guards. . . .

Total amount of damage sustained since commencement of the war: $543,743.46.

On the 4th of July, 1863 the advance guard of Morgan's command appeared near Lebanon, burned Hardin's Creek bridge, and made an attempt to capture a train at St. Mary's, but were repulsed by the train guard. One soldier, a passenger on the train, was killed in this attack. On the 5th of July, Morgan captured Lebanon, after an obstinate fight with the Federal force; the depot buildings and engine house at that place were completely destroyed and the cars in the depot yard burned. On the 6th of July Morgan, on his way to the North of the Ohio, crossed the main stem of the road at Bardstown Junction, captured a passenger train there, which he afterwards released, and burned the bridge over Long Lick, together with the adjoining tank house.

Since that time no large organized forces have been on the road, but we have suffered considerable losses from small bands of guerrillas, whose object is less to interfere with the operations of the road than to rob the passengers and trains, and to gratify their love for wanton destruction. On the 4th of July, the depot at Rocky Hill, which had just been rebuilt, was again burned by such a band. On the 28th of July, three freight cars were burned at Allensville. On the 25th of September, the bridge over Nolin River was set on fire, but was saved from total destruction by some of the neighbors. The damage was soon repaired. On the first of October, the Depot at Auburn, containing a large amount of Government corn was burned. On October 7th, Capt. Richardson's gang captured the Lebanon train, and burned two passenger cars, and one baggage car. On the 28th of October, the Bardstown train was captured, one passenger car and one baggage car burned, and the locomotive badly injured. . . .

These attacks of robber bands interfere most seriously with keeping on the line of the road sufficient force to do the required work. Our men have frequently been robbed of their money, clothes, watches, and their lives have been threatened in case they should continue to work for the Company. The military authorities have, as yet, not been able to break up these gangs of robbers, and as long as they are permitted to commit such depredations, the difficulties of operating the road will continue.

The total amount of damage done to the road since the commencement of the war will appear from the following statement:

Amount expended previous to July 1, 1863 $440,570.31
Amount expended fiscal year, ending July 1, 1864 $ 60,735.26
To be expended after July 1, 1864 $119,145.00

During this year many locomotives and cars were taken by the Federal authorities under orders from the military forces, seriously interfering with the transportation of passengers and property over the road.

Year ending June 30, 1865—There were in operation 60 locomotives, 42 passenger cars, 9 baggage cars, 8 express cars, 295 box cars, 104 rack cars, 21 gondola cars, 107 flat cars, 70 gravel and stone cars and 12 boarding cars. . . .

The amount of damage done by Confederate forces and guerrillas to the Company's property during the past year is . . . $94,346.45. On the 20th of August 1864, the depot at Woodburn, only reconstructed a short time before, was again destroyed by guerrillas. On the 1st of September, the Lebanon passenger train was captured near New Hope, and the baggage car destroyed. On the 12th of September, a gang of guerrillas captured the Bardstown train and burned one passenger car. . . . On October 21st—a freight train captured near Rich Pond: eight of the Company's cars, besides two Adams Express and Government cars were destroyed, and engine No. 161 was badly damaged. . . . December 16th— Guerrillas burned one span of Rolling Fork bridge, near New Haven, together with four cars, with which they set fire to the bridge. Lyon's forces burned the bridge over Nolin River, and the depot at Elizabethtown, which had been rebuilt but a short time previously. They also burned part of the bridge over Valley Creek, near Elizabethtown, captured a passenger train, and destroyed three passenger cars, one baggage and one express car. January 6th, 1865—Magruder captured a construction train at Lebanon Junction. He ran the engine into a wood train, broke up four cars, and burned one car loaded with hay, and standing on the side track. . . .

The amount of money expended during the year in restoring the Company's property destroyed during the war . . . $ 87,288.03
    Amount expended prior to July 1, 1864   501,593.60
    Total amount of damage sustained   688,372.56

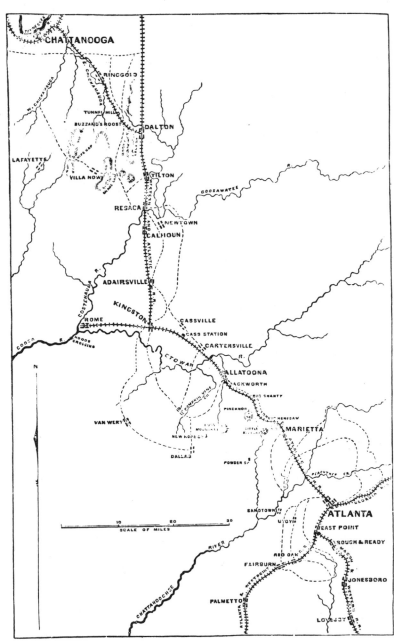

Figure 6. Map of the Western & Atlantic Railroad, April 1864, from Atlanta to Chattanooga, the route of the chase of the *General.*

The "Great Locomotive Chase"

The "Great Locomotive Chase," or the Andrews Raid, has been the most often described exploit in railroad history. In April, 1862, a Union spy named James J. Andrews, led twenty-one men through the Confederate lines to Marietta, Georgia, where they captured a railroad engine, the *General*. They ran it northward towards Chattanooga, Tennessee, destroying telegraph communication as they went. But Confederate troops, in another engine, the *Texas*, pursued the *General* and caught it after an exciting chase. The Confederates hanged Andrews and seven of his men.

Figure 6 maps the route of the chase, and Figures 7 through 14 show scenes along the line, including some of Wilbur Kurtz's paintings. One of these shows the *William Smith* at Kingston Station, an engine involved slightly in the chase but seldom mentioned or pictured.

ALLATOONA PASS.[1]

BLOCK-HOUSE AT CHATTANOOGA.

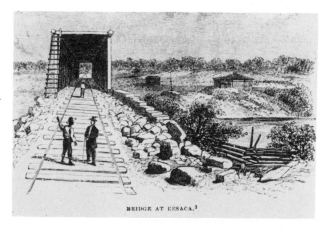

BRIDGE AT RESACA.[3]

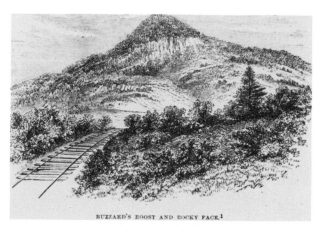

BUZZARD'S ROOST AND ROCKY FACE.[1]

Figure 7.   Scenes along the Western & Atlantic line.

Figure 8. Allatoona Pass, 1864.

Figure 9. The *Yonah* at Etowah Station (Wilbur Kurtz painting).

Figure 10. Cass Station.

Figure 11. The *Wm. Smith* at Kingston Station (Wilbur Kurtz painting).

Figure 12. Tunnel Hill Station. New tunnel in the distance, original tunnel at right.

Figure 13. Ringgold Station from the south; compare it with the plan. It was partially rebuilt in 1910. New stonework at left replaces the corner damaged by a shell.

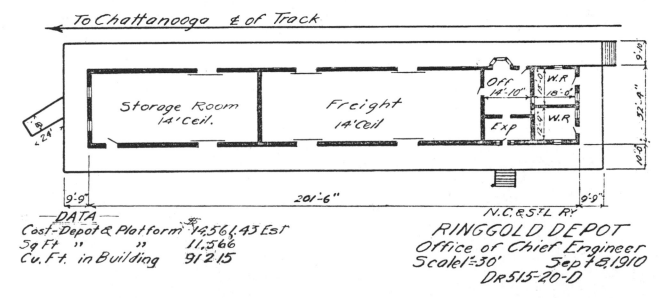

Figure 14. *Top:* War sketch of Ringgold Station. The building was much larger, according to N. C. & St. L. R. R. plan below.

Long Bridge, Washington

At the beginning of the war the longest approach to Washington was the famous Long Bridge, a mile in length, connecting the national capital with Alexandria, Virginia, the gateway to the confederacy. Three earthen forts commanded the entrance. The photograph in Figure 15 represents one of the first pictures taken by Matthew Brady, showing a sentry on duty and the sergeant of the guard ready to examine the pass. No man ever crossed Long Bridge without this written oath:

> *It is understood that the within named and subscriber accepts this pass on his word of honor that he is and will be ever loyal to the United States; and if hereafter found in the arms against the Union, or in any way aiding her enemies, the penalty will be death.*

The Long Bridge had been built in 1809. In 1855 Congress authorized the Alexandria and Washington Railroad, whose track ended at the bridge, to lay a rail connection in Washington to the Baltimore & Ohio station. Omnibuses and wagons were used for crossing the bridge. Later the Virginia trackage was removed.

At the outbreak of hostilities the War Department took possession of Long Bridge. Thomas A. Scott of the Pennsylvania Railroad came to Washington April 26, 1861, to

Figure 15.   The original Long Bridge across the Potomac at Washington; note the disused rails. New railroad bridge is at left. View is toward the Virginia shore.

Figure 16. *Left:* The original Long Bridge. *Right:* The new railroad bridge at the ship's channel Virginia end (length 5,104 feet). An **A**-frame with cables supported the movable span.

organize railroad and telegraphic communications for the War Department under Simon Cameron, its secretary. Cognizant of the importance of rail connections to the south, one of Scott's first acts was to have rails laid across the bridge and to Alexandria. Crews completed the project by working day and night for seven days.

Because of its increasing military role, traffic improvement was imperative and the secretary of war ordered the bridge rebuilt, strengthening and widening it with the addition of a single track. The work was finished February 1, 1862. Col. D. C. McCallum's report of September 23, 1863, says, "The Washington and Alexandria has been in daily use since Feb. 1, 1862, as the main communication between the railroads north and south of Washington and Long Bridge across the Potomac River is used as a part of it and kept in repair also for the other purposes by the Military Railroad." In 1863 Congress authorized the Washington and Alexandria Railroad to build an additional structure along the east side of the bridge for its own uses and to be operated as a military railroad. In 1870 the bridge was taken over by the Baltimore and Potomac Railroad.

CHAPTER II
Track Construction: Actual & Scale

AT THE BEGINNING OF THE 1860s, track and roadbed were not yet, except for a very few larger railroads, what might be defined as standard. Rail was mostly of the so-called pear-section type, roughly similar to what would soon be called T rail. But much more primitive track existed, such as inverted U rails (Figure 27), especially in the South and on the Louisville & Chattanooga, where wooden stringers were often used under each rail. Stringers under the ties, parallel to the rails, were common and were known as mud sills, because most of the South's railroads used earth, sand, or gravel for ballast, which helped slightly for stiffening. A fair amount of strap-iron-on-stringer trackage was in use and even some stone block roadbed still existed.

All rails were iron; the first steel rails were not rolled until 1867, by the Cambria Iron Company in Pennsylvania. The pear-shaped rails weighed 45 to 65 pounds per yard and were 3 to 3½ inches high. U rails weighed about 42 pounds per yard and came in lengths as short as 6 feet. Lengths of most types of rails up to 1850 were 15, 16, and 18 feet, by 1857 were 21, 24, and 27 feet long, and by 1860 to 1865 reached 30 feet in length.

Various types of bars to splice rails were in use, U-shaped plates around the base of the rail similar to what model railroaders call joiners or short iron bars inside the rail with wooden stringers 4 feet long outside. These were known as Trimble splices. Most of the largest eastern railroads, such as the Pennsylvania, the New York Central and Hudson River, the Camden and Amboy, the Baltimore & Ohio, and the Central Railroad of New Jersey used these. They can be seen in many photos (Figure 20) and were first mentioned in print in a report by the New York Board of Commissioners in 1856.

Ties were not nearly as well finished as those used in later years, often being logs averaging 6 to 8 inches in diameter and varying from 8 to 10 feet 2 inches in length, with one side faced off to take the rails. Most were not treated with a preservative, although this had been tried as early as the 1830s and larger roads in the North were beginning to make the process standard. Ballast consisted of whatever was handiest; only the more affluent railroads like the Pennsylvania and the New York Central went to the expense of using crushed stone on their main lines.

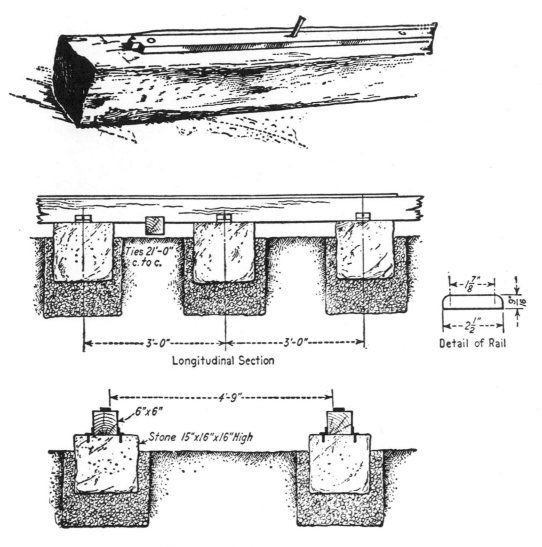

Ties 21'-0" c. to c.

3'-0"   3'-0"

Longitudinal Section

1 7/8"   9/16"   2 1/2"

Detail of Rail

4'-9"

6"x6"

Stone 15"x16"x16"High

Transverse Section

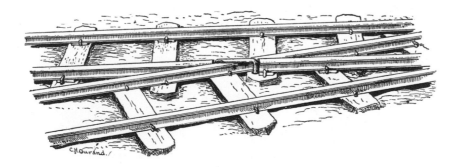

Figure 17. *Top:* Iron strap rail on timber. *Middle:* Strap rail as laid on stone block roadbed. *Bottom:* An early switch showing the use of a staple (U) inverted in place of a frog.

Figure 18. A model switch.

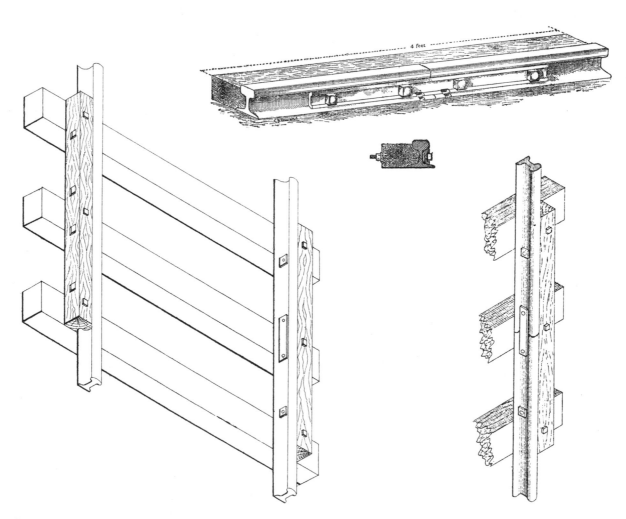

Figure 19. The Trimble splice, a standard type used by the Baltimore & Ohio, Pennsylvania, New York Central & Hudson River, and New Jersey railroads in the early 1860s. A four-foot timber outside the rail as illustrated bolted through a narrow iron bar inside provided ample stiffening.

Figure 20.   Above: Pennsylvania Railroad track with Trimble joints at Greensburg, Pa. *Below:* Pennsylvania track at Gallitzin. Note the switch stand.

Figure 21. A three-way stub switch on the Pennsylvania at Altoona.

Switches were of the stub type; it would be another ten years before the point type supplanted them. Before frogs were used as part of switch construction, various devices were used (Figures 17 and 18). A variety of switch stands (Figures 20, 22, and 23) were in use, but many switches were operated by a simple ground lever with a weighted arm. Lanterns on switch stands were generally unknown until the 1870s. No signals were used in the South, nor were there many in the North, according to Wilbur Kurtz, probably the best authority on Southern railroads of the period. Not until the 1870s are they to be seen in photographs of Northern roads. Train operations were controlled by telegraph on most if not all roads in the North and South. Telegraph poles seen in photographs or sketches of the Civil War period usually had one insulator, except perhaps in busier areas. Crossarms on poles seldom appear until the 1870s. Often the wires were hung from the undersides of these, frequently without insulators and on hooks.

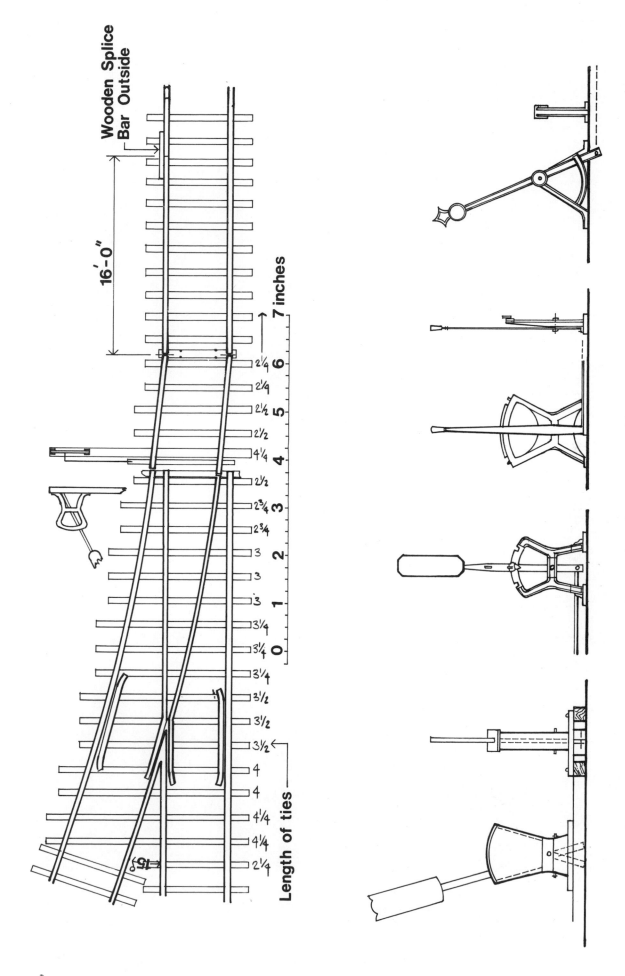

Figure 22. Above: Construction of a model ¼-scale stub switch and types of early switch stands.

Figure 23. Remains of the Richmond & Petersburg Railroad bridge at Richmond; note switch stands. For a view of the bridge before its destruction see Figure 72.

Figure 24. Three-way stub switches and switch stands on the Philadelphia, Wilmington and Baltimore at the entrance to the Susquehanna River Ferry at Havre de Grace, Maryland. A bridge 3,269 feet in length was opened for traffic November 28, 1866, completing an all-rail line between Philadelphia and Baltimore.

As the war continued and the supply of rail became critical in the South, less important roads and branch lines were stripped of their rails to help maintain the more important arteries. In some cases it was necessary to resort to the old strap-iron-and-stringer construction. Figure 25 shows such track being torn up by Sherman's troops after leaving Atlanta.

Figure 25.   Union troops tearing up strap rail track. The location is not identified.

Figure 26.   Union soldiers tearing up a more standard track.

Figure 27.   An old-type U-rail, an early switch lever,
probably prestand type, and a very early type of frog.

Modeling Civil War Railroads

There are at least two basic approaches to modeling the railroads and equipment of the Civil War period. One is to plan and construct an operating railroad in a given space, to fit a room or a portion of a room. The other, which would perhaps take more planning, is to build and combine a number of scenes to be made separately and installed as components of an operating model system. In a sense it would be similar to what museums do: everything would not be continuously on display, but exhibits would be varied from time to time. Thus, the many photographs of scenes in this book might suggest similar ones to be built in miniature in the workroom or shop and then moved into location. For example, the locomotive *General* pursued by the *Texas* might run through several scenes created and based on Figures 7 through 14 in Chapter I.

The first decision to be made concerns the scale to be used. That of ¼" = 1'0" (O gauge track) is suggested for modeling these early railroads and their equipment as well as that of the years just before and after them. The engines and cars of those times were small: 4-4-0 types in this scale would average no more than 12 inches including the tender, and passenger cars actually 60 feet long would scale out at 15 inches. Consequently, much-smaller-radius curves can be used than would be necessary for models of large modern equipment, as little as 24-inch radius, but preferably 30 or 36 inches. Thus, even less space is required for this early period by modeling in O gauge than large modern steam locomotives require in HO gauge. The smaller engines and passenger cars require more decorative finishing, and this too is better accomplished with the results more easily appreciated in ¼" scale.

Rail and track are other considerations. In scale the code .100 rail used for HO-gauge track is close in size and scale to the small rails of the 1860s in O gauge. Obviously, most existing HO track is oversized in scale if used for 1860s modeling. There are also more adaptable ¼"-scale components for locomotives and cars, as well as structures, than in the smaller scale, and more are being developed.

It is, of course, always up to the individual hobbyist to make his own choice as to which scale or gauge he prefers. I think that for the various reasons mentioned ¼" scale has the advantage for this kind of miniature work.

PLANNING THE LAYOUT

As already mentioned, planning the railroad ahead is most important. A fundamental design and layout must be decided upon, regardless of the construction method. The railroad should be a single-track line with passing and dead-end sidings as desired or necessary. Considering the military aspects, locations for batteries (field guns), supplies and stores, camps, or other facilities should be provided. The terrain would be generally hilly, as most photographs of the period show, so a tunnel or two might be included. However, level areas should be located for the elements mentioned, for farmland, and for building sites. If space permits, part of a navigable river with a wharf and supply depot might be interesting (see Chapter XIII) as well as a small engine house, shop and turntable.

Other than military features, there should of course be a small station with a few buildings, anything that seems appropriate. Models of such a scene and drawings for

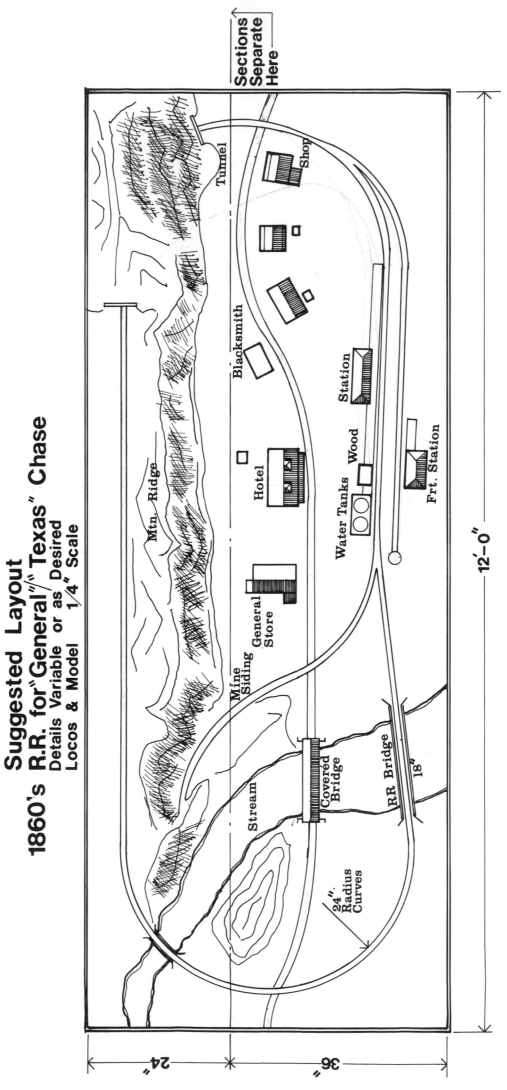

Suggested Layout
1860's R.R. for "General" / "Texas" Chase
Details Variable or as Desired
Locos & Model 1/4" Scale

Sections Separate Here

Tunnel

Shop

Blacksmith

Station

Mtn. Ridge

Hotel

Wood

Water Tanks

Frt. Station

General Store

Mine Siding

Stream

Covered Bridge

R.R. Bridge

18"

24" Radius Curves

12'-0"

24"

36"

Figure 28. Suggested plan for a small 1/4"-scale layout.

various buildings may be seen in Chapter III. They indicate some possibilities, but the many photographs herein are intended to suggest others.

TRACK CONSTRUCTION

The project, then, is a historical, scenic, working model railroad, only distantly related to toy trains. It might be called a three-dimensional painting, and as such everything must be to scale and adhere faithfully to the period it depicts. Starting with track, there is presently nothing one can purchase readymade that will represent that of the 1860s. Rail (code. 100) is available, as well as frogs and spikes, but from this point on track will have to be handmade.

Ties in ¼″ scale should be ⅛″ to ³⁄₁₆″ square, or thinner to suggest their being partly buried in ballast. The ³⁄₁₆″ size is preferable, representing a 9″ timber. The lengths should vary from 2″ to 2½″. Basswood or pine is recommended and is available from at least two sources and some hobby stores. But if a Civil War model railroad is built with ties made of this strip wood it would look too perfect. The various photos in this chapter show different lengths and types of ties. To simulate them a number of others cut from twigs should be interspersed here and there among the standard ones. Any small branches with twigs about ³⁄₁₆″ or a shade larger in diameter can be used, but they must be thoroughly dry before cutting them to varying lengths and then filed or sanded smooth on opposite sides. Note in old photos that the ends are not saw cut but hand hewn with axes.

A medium brown to gray water soluble paint can be used for dying the basswood and natural ties.

Well-dried dark earth will do for ballast, but it should be sifted. If foundry sand is obtainable it might be preferable, for it is much finer than ordinary sand.

Ties can be spaced farther apart than modern spacing—a scale 18″ or a bit more.

Trimble splices (Figures 19 and 20) are easy to simulate. Use 1″ pieces of ³⁄₃₂″ basswood strips outside the rails that have been notched slightly on the head to represent 30-foot lengths, 7½″ in ¼″ scale. The inner iron plates are so small that they might be forgotten unless the builder is a purist.

Rubber cement is suggested for putting the ties on the roadbed. Brush the cement on the roadbed for about 6 inches, set ties in place, and then sprinkle ballast on. One must work fast, as this cement sets quickly, but it has the advantage of allowing easy changes in ties and the like. When ties and ballast have set, brush off the surplus ballast.

A typical stub switch is shown in scale (Figure 22) and is simple to build. It may be necessary to build the frog from rail if the radius of the curve is less than 3 feet, which is about the smallest available in castings. At least one of the types of switch stands illustrated is available, but construction of others is not difficult. The usual insulation for two-rail operation should be done at switches, as in standard two-rail track. For remote control, switch machines can be hidden under the baseboard with the switchstand there only for appearance.

Figure 29. The old Frederick station on the B & O opened Dec. 2, 1831.

CHAPTER III
Railroad Structures

AS NECESSARY ADJUNCTS TO ANY RAILROAD, big or small, stations come first in importance. In the first thirty years of railroading most depots were plain, utilitarian, and adequate for the facilities then provided. Most of those existing in 1860 were, with a few exceptions, good examples of simple construction, making their duplication in miniature relatively easy. One of the earliest, the station at Frederick, Maryland, on the B & O, may be seen in Figure 29.

Ordinarily, when building a model station a wall is laid out with the door and window locations on a single piece of wood, then these openings are cut out. But an easier way, using ¼″-thick basswood, is to cut a piece for the lower part of the wall up to the windows, another the height of the windows, and a third top section from the windows to the roof line. Piecing together the bottom, window "spacers," and top this way makes wall construction simpler. A variety of plastic doors and windows are available to complete it.

If the wall is clapboard, batten, or brick, basswood milled to represent the first two is available, as is plastic sheet impressed for bricks also. If, however, the wall is to look like stone, the use of a flexible dental shaft and fine round burrs to outline the pointing of the masonry is suggested. It does take time to do scores or more "stones," but it is worth it. Paint the individual stones in a variety of grays and browns; one solid color is too uniform.

The model station in Figure 33 was built from drawings developed from an original on the old Cincinnati Southern Railway, but it is shortened a bit. As the model neared completion it was found that the roof overhang of a scale 8 feet (2″) was so much that people, luggage, and detail on the platform were not easily seen, so the overhang was cut back one inch as the photographs of the model show. Over five hundred pieces of basswood went into this model, but the construction could be simplified by using scribed wood instead of individual pieces.

Roof material representing several kinds of such covering is available in pressed plastic sheets. As an adhesive for most small model building construction water soluble glue is not recommended, because assemblies are liable to warp. Most acetate or acetone cements are preferable.

The turntable in Figure 36 is an interesting as well as useful structure, and this one, which was at Manassas Junction, is different from familiar designs. The drawings were developed from the photograph and the model (Figure 39) resulted. It is 12 inches long, ample to accommodate most old 4-4-0 locomotives, and the diameter of the circular rail is 11 inches. Basswood is the principal material used.

Figure 30. Annapolis Junction, Maryland, where the new Washington branch connected with the B & O. Service was inaugurated July 20, 1835.

Figure 31. A ¼″-scale model of the first station in Harrisburg, Pa. Model by the author, authentic background painting by Ranulph Bye.

Figure 32. Two early Pennsylvania stations in the 1860s. *Left:* East Liberty. *Right:* Shadyside.

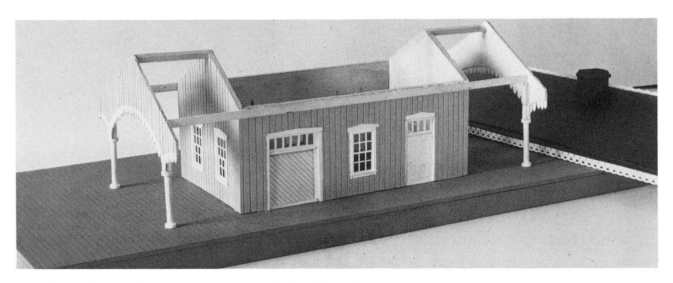

Figure 33.   A Southern station modeled in ¼″ scale.

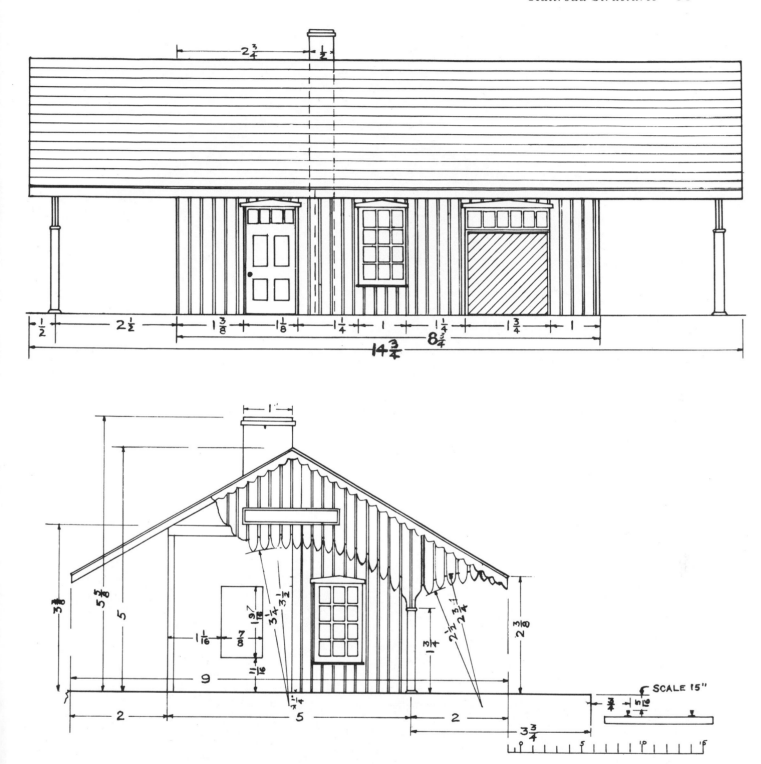

Figure 34. Side and end elevations for the model station (⅛″ scale).

Figure 35. Another somewhat similar Southern-type station, at Dahlgren, Illinois, on the Louisville & Nashville's Lewiston–St. Louis line.

Figure 36. The turntable at Manassas Junction, Virginia, after the battle of Bull Run. The Manassas Gap Railroad joined the Orange & Alexandria Railroad at this point.

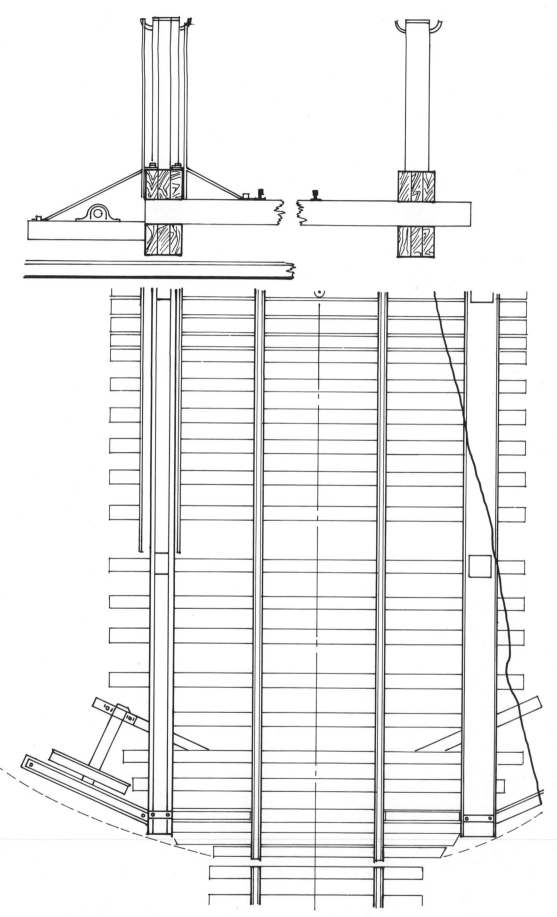

Figure 37.   Plan and section in ¼″ scale of the Manassas Junction turntable.

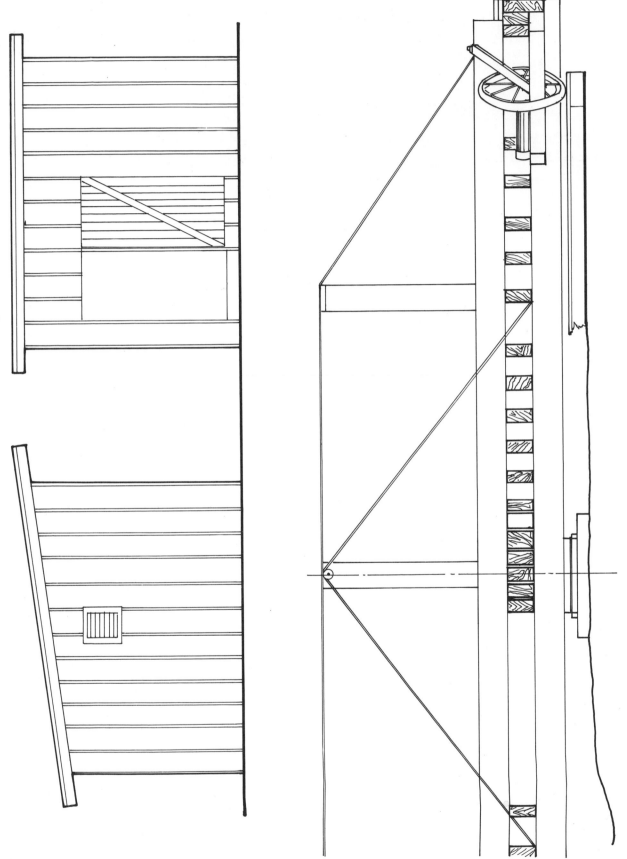

Figure 38. Below: Side elevation of the reconstruction model turntable in ¼″ scale. *Above:* ¼″-scale drawing of a small tool shed.

Figure 39. The finished model built from the foregoing plans.

The several drawings of water tanks provide the dimensions in ¼″ scale. A cylinder or the piece of tubing, 3 ³⁄₆″ in diameter, that masking tape comes on works out very well for the tank, but the size could vary. Strips of ⅛″ basswood ¹⁄₃₂″ or ¹⁄₁₆″ thick cemented on vertically give the effect of wooden construction. The rest of the assembly is evident.

Figure 40. A twin water tank at Union Mills on the Orange & Alexandria Railroad. The trains are picking up debris after the second battle of Bull Run.

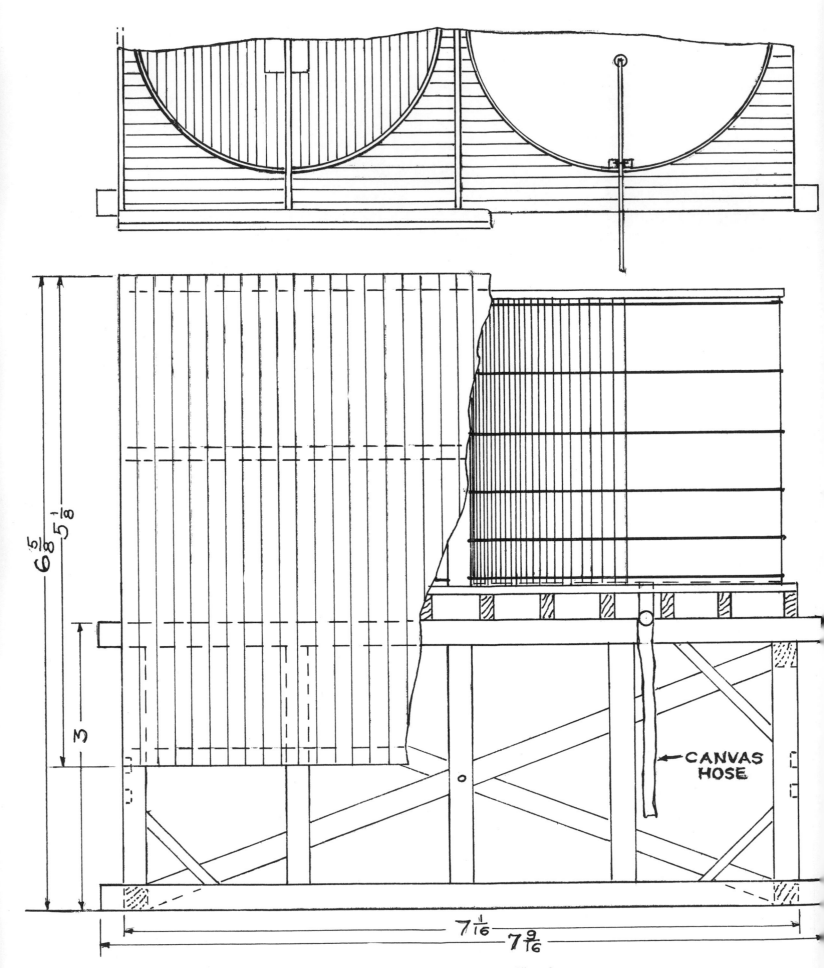

Figure 41. Plan and side elevation of twin water tank with front siding, ¼″ scale.

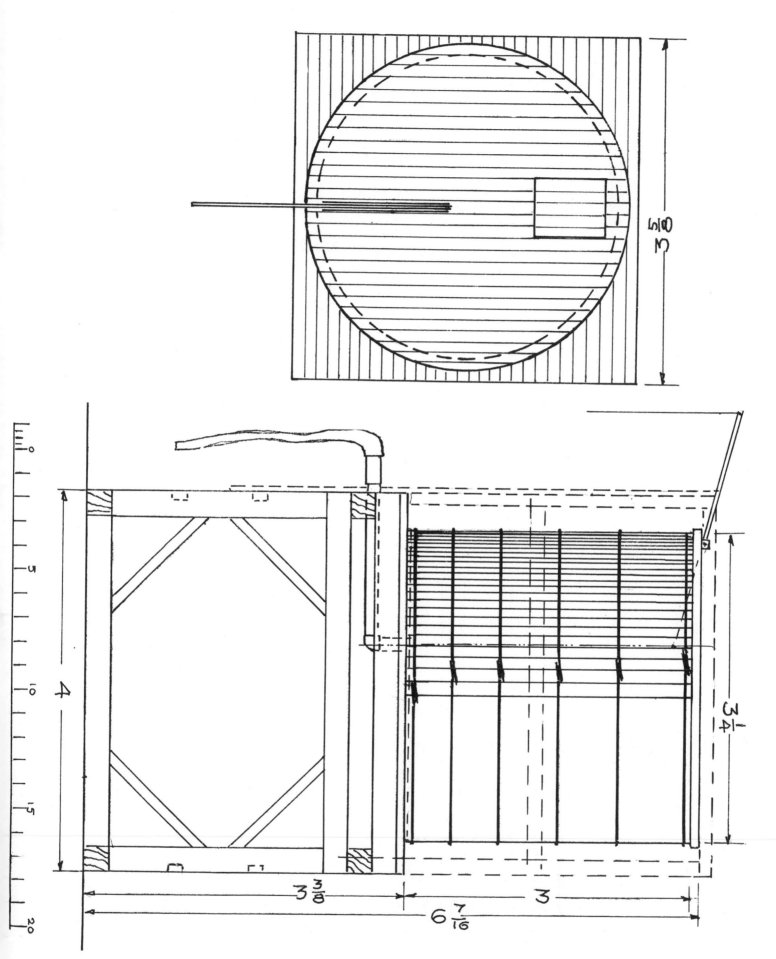

Figure 42. Plan and elevation of a single water tank, ¼" scale.

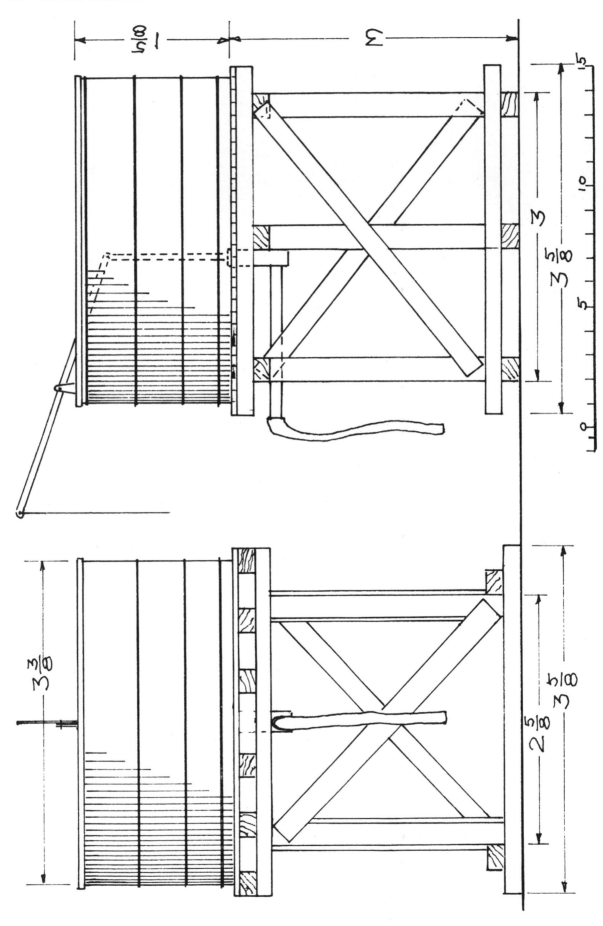

Figure 43. Plan and elevation of a smaller tank, ¼" scale.

Figure 44. A standpipe and platform on the Pennsylvania Railroad at Millerstown, Pa.

Water standpipes were simple, upright pipes with an elbow fitted with a piece of firehose. A valve at ground level was usual until later when a valve that the fireman could reach from the tender top was made. A more elaborate type is that which the Pennsylvania Railroad used (Figure 44); Figure 45 supplies the dimensions. A piece of flat white shoelace simulates the hose.

A large rectangular water tank was used at the Alexandria engine house, but the same general design was also used elsewhere (Figures 46 and 47).

As most fuel in those days was wood, open or covered ricks held the supply, and stops to replenish the tender were frequent. Two types are shown in Figures 48 and 49. Much larger facilities for storing wood were used on larger roads such as the ones that may be seen at the Millerstown station of the Pennsylvania, in Figure 53.

Engine houses were built of wood, brick, or stone. On many small railroads or branch lines they were rectangular in shape and often only large enough for two engines. On more important roads roundhouses were common, only some being completely circular, surrounding a turntable in the center. Figure 50 shows an old roundhouse segment with a

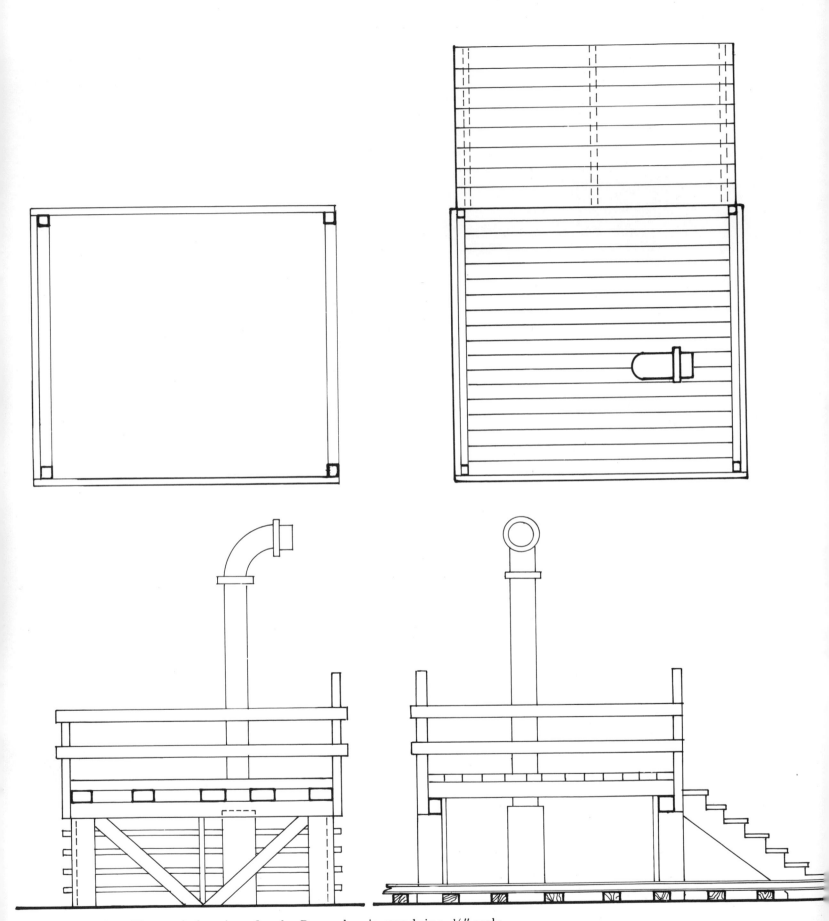

Figure 45. Plan and elevations for the Pennsylvania standpipe, ¼″ scale.

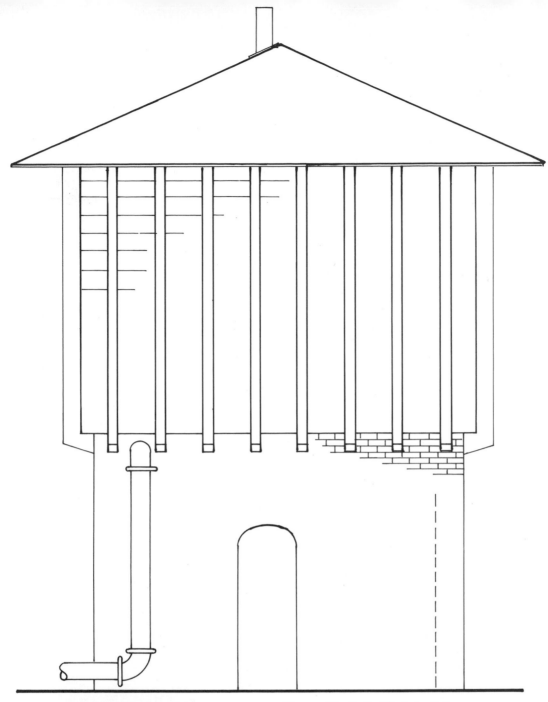

Figure 46. Left: Model of the
small-capacity water tank, ¼″ scale.
Above: End elevation of the rectangular
water tank at Alexandria, ¼″ scale.

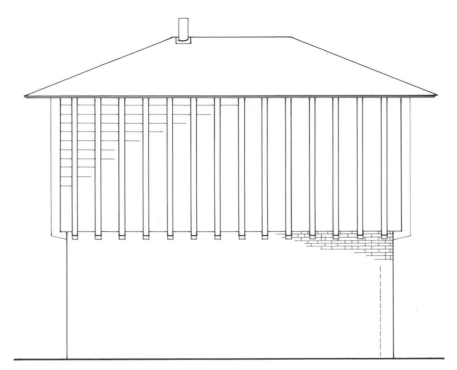

Figure 47. Side elevation of the Alexandria water tank.

Figure 48. *Above:* A model of a covered wood rick.
Opposite: Drawings of an uncovered wood rick.

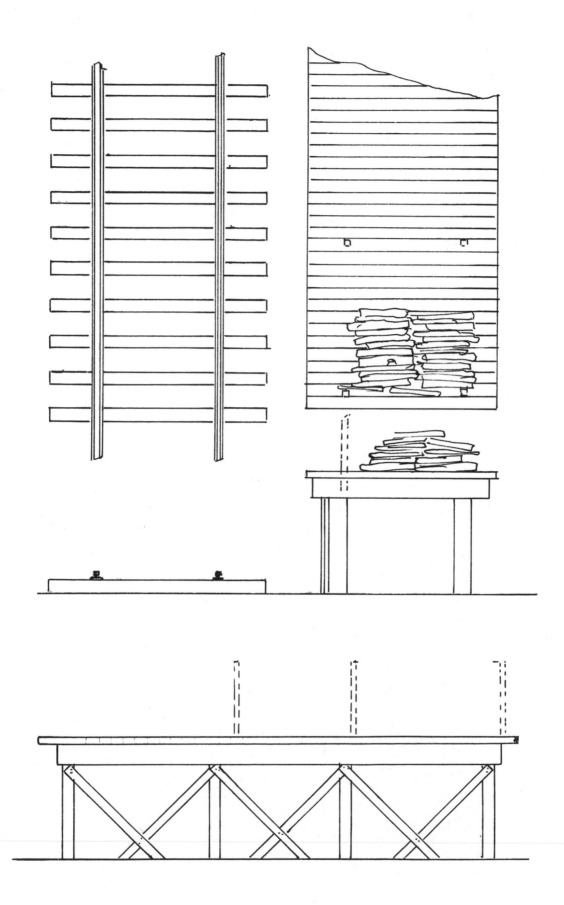

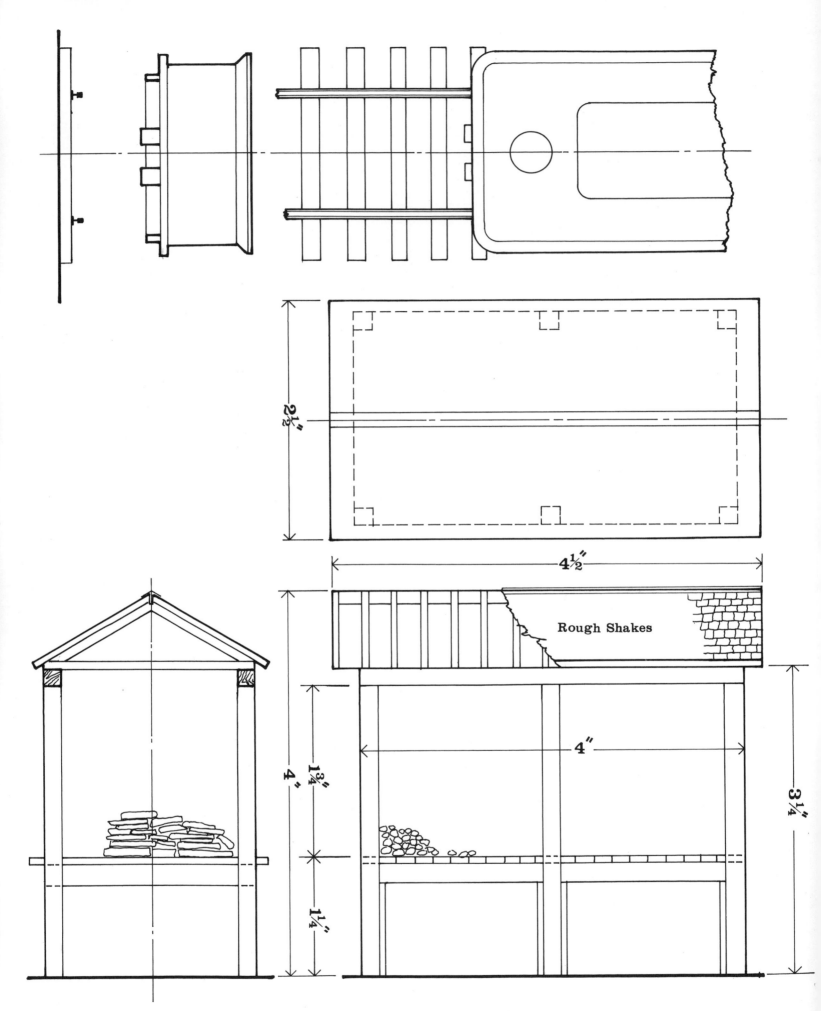

Figure 49. Plan and elevations ¼″ scale, of a covered wood rick.

Figure 50. An old stone two-stall engine house at Flemington, New Jersey, on the Pennsylvania Railroad. Note single smoke jack.

turntable and only two engine stalls, which evidently serviced only one, however, because there was only one smoke jack. The elevations (Figure 51) were proportioned for the model (Figure 52). The stone finish was achieved by hand carving with a small dental burr.

Old plans of engine house and shop facilities for the Richmond and Allegheny Railroad, the forerunner of the Chesapeake & Ohio, are illustrated in Figures 53, 54, and 55. They suggest how design and architecture may be adapted for a smaller model installation.

More scenes for modeling may be found in Figures 56–58.

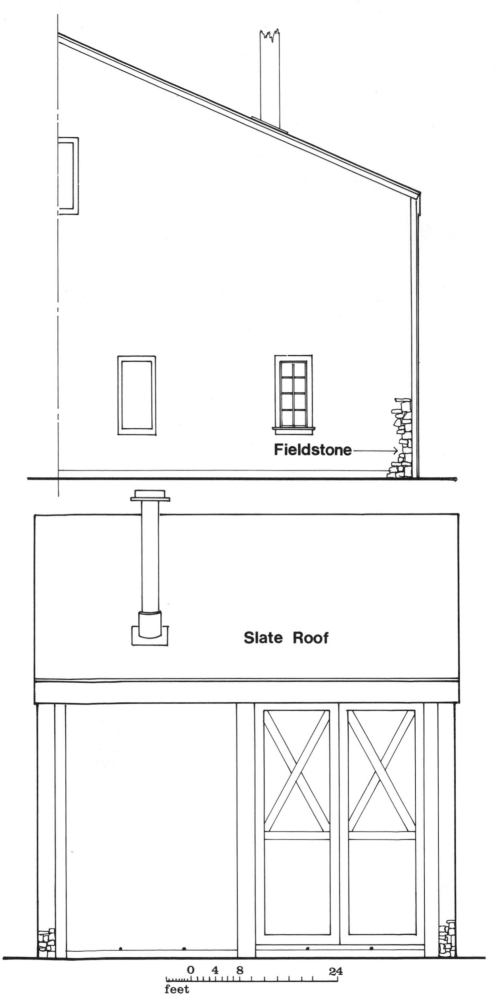

Fieldstone

Slate Roof

0 4 8   24
feet

Figure 51.   Elevations of the stone engine house; scale indicated.

Figure 52. Model of the old engine house, ¼″ scale.

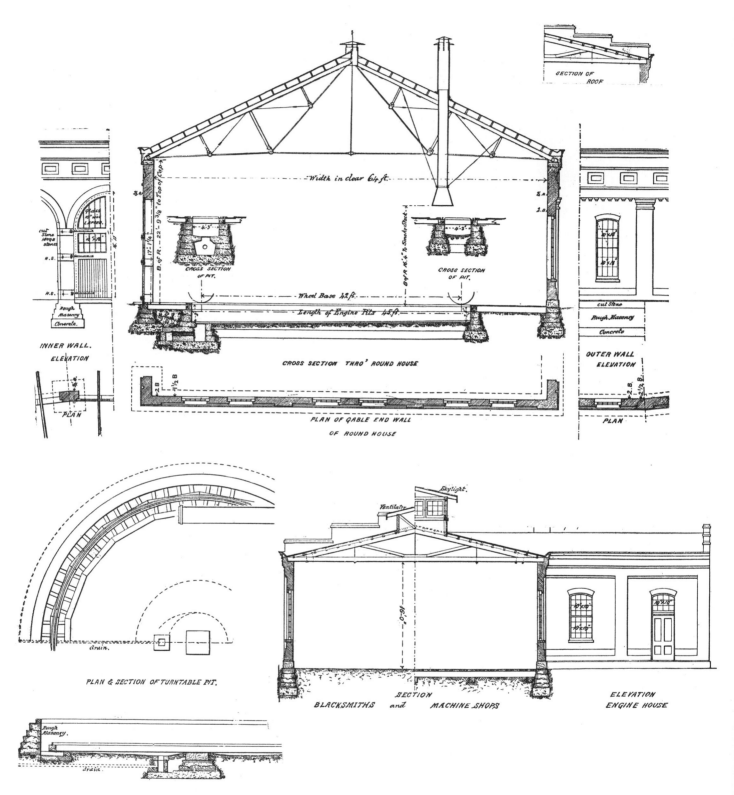

Figure 53. Old drawings of roundhouse and shops of the Richmond and Alleghany Railroad at Richmond, Virginia. Various scales.

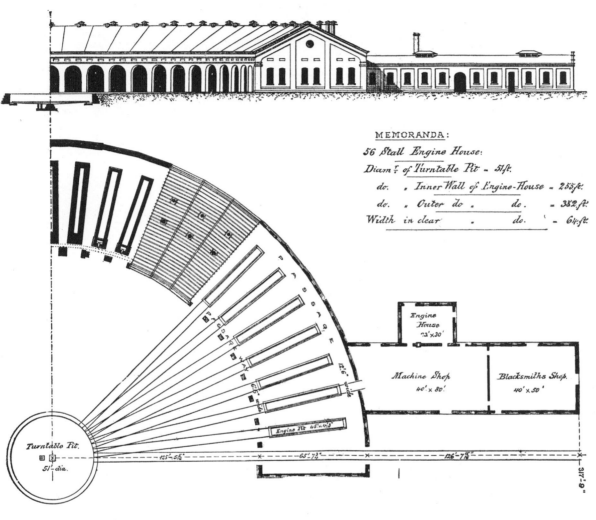

MEMORANDA:

56 Stall Engine House:

Diam. of Turntable Pit - 51 ft.

do. „ Inner Wall of Engine-House = 255 ft.

do. „ Outer do „ do. = 382 ft.

Width in clear . do. - 64 ft.

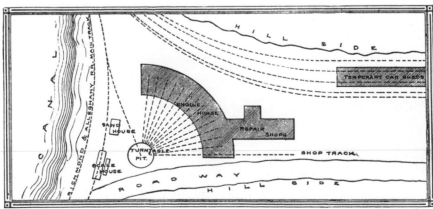

Figure 54. Plan and elevations for the drawings in Figure 53. Various scales.

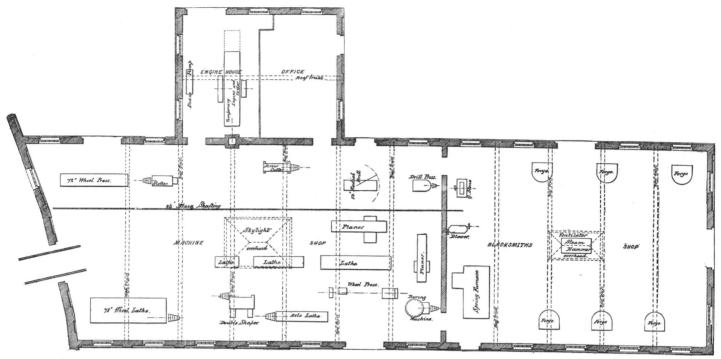

Figure 55. Plan of repair shop of the Richmond and Alleghany Railroad at Richmond, Virginia.

Figure 56. Roundhouse at Petersburg, Virginia. Boxcar lettering at left, "P. & W. R. R. Petersburg, Virginia." *Center:* Rear of tender *Confederate States. Right, center:* Four-wheel gondola "No. 2 P. R. R. Co." *Foreground, right:* Part of boxcar. "C. S. A." Note Union soldiers (*left*), locomotive bell on roof, three smokestacks on flatcar.

Figure 57. Memphis & Charleston Railroad yard at Memphis. Boxcar at left is from East Tennessee, Virginia & Georgia Railroad.

Figure 58. The train shed at Chattanooga, somewhat similar to that at Atlanta on the Western & Atlantic Railroad.

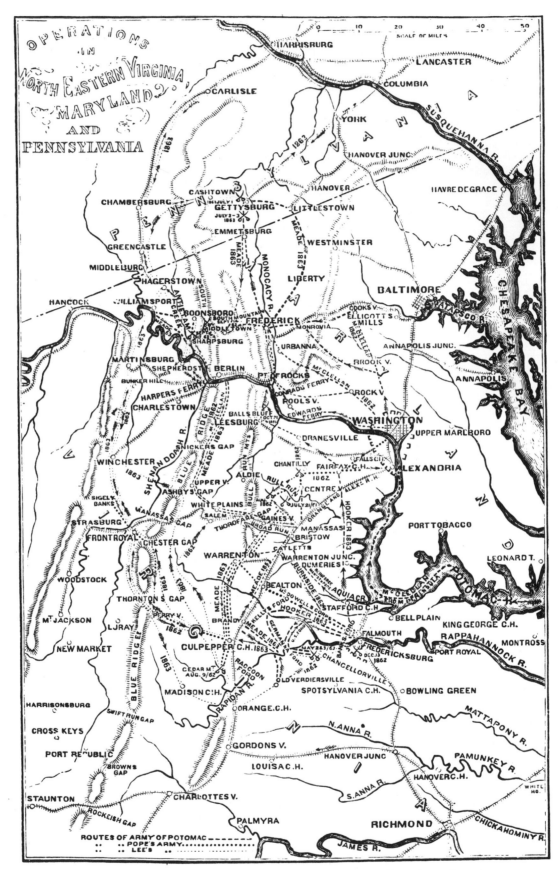

Figure 59. Map, summer of 1863, locating various railroads and towns west of Washington and Alexandria and north of Richmond.

CHAPTER IV
Nonrailroad Structures

THE DRAWINGS in this chapter are sketched and scaled from a selection of old photographs of buildings, mostly in eastern Virginia in the 1860s. In several cases the models built from these sketches are shown. The basic materials mentioned in the preceding chapter were again used.

A variation in construction might be to build a small arch bridge in actual masonry. A model done this way about twenty-five years ago is shown in Figure 80b. Selecting the small stones is important, as the tendency is to use larger than scale size. In ¼″ scale, none of the stones should exceed ¾″ and preferably not be larger than ½″ by a lesser thickness. A sheet-metal form for the arch (either in location on the layout or, better, made on the bench), a small batch of fine cement, and perhaps more than a bit of patience are the other ingredients. A small dental spatula would be helpful, too. A larger bridge with two arches over Antietam Creek is shown in Figure 63.

A small covered road bridge is included with a railroad covered bridge drawing in Chapter V, Figure 79. The construction, as always, is of basswood.

Figure 60. View of gristmill at Fredericksburg on the Rappahannock, 1863. Confederate troops watch photographer across destroyed railroad bridge.

Figure 61. A ¼″-scale model of an eighteenth-century stone farmhouse in Pennsylvania. Model by the author, 1940.

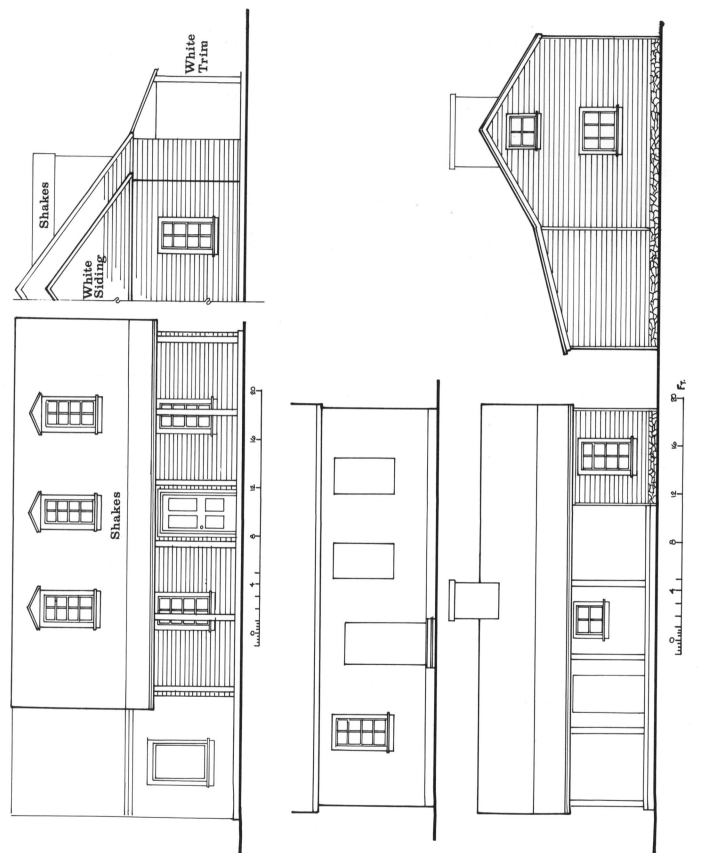

Shakes

White Siding

White Trim

Shakes

Ft.

Figure 62. *Above:* A ⅛″-scale drawing of a tavern at Poolesville, Maryland. *Below:* Also in ⅛″ scale, elevations of the tavern and of the Centreville farmhouse.

Figure 63. Above: The stone bridge over Antietam Creek between Boonesboro and Sharpsburg, site of battle September 16 and 17, 1862. *Below, left:* Another tavern. *Right:* A house at Knoxville, Tennessee.

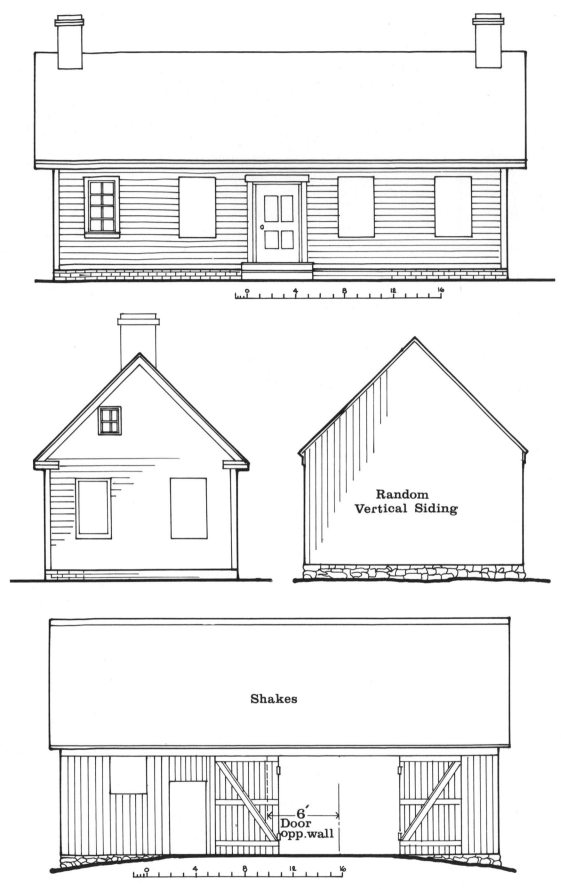

Random Vertical Siding

Shakes

6'
Door
opp. wall

Figure 64. Above: A ⅛″-scale elevation of front of a farmhouse near Chattanooga. *Middle:* The end of the farmhouse and of a barn to accompany it. *Below:* Front of barn.

Figure 65. Models in ¼″ scale of the farmhouse and barn.

Figure 66a. Model of stone arch bridge.

Figure 66b. Drawing of a town or city building, a bakery at Georgetown next to the Forest Hall Military Prison, Washington; ⅛″ scale.

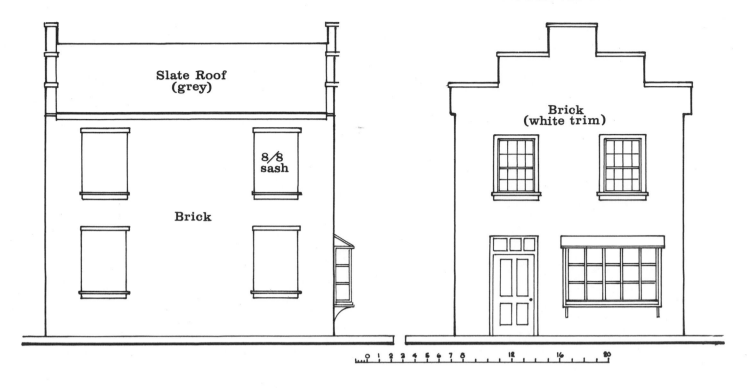

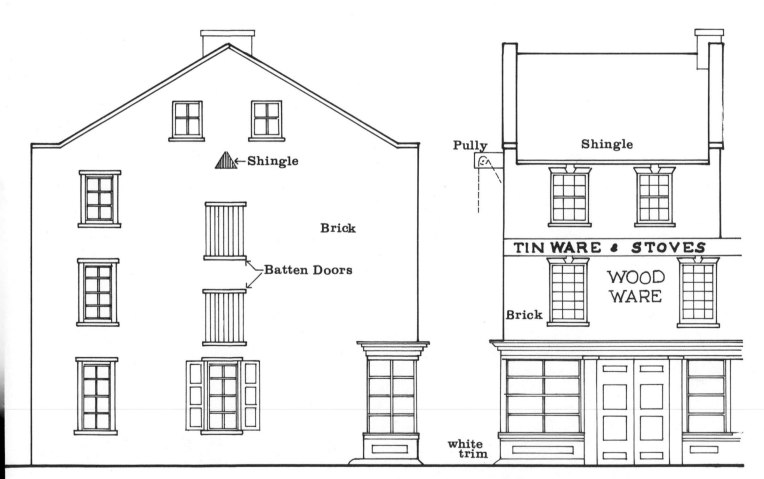

Figure 67. *Above:* Drawings of a corner building in Culpeper, Virginia. *Below:* A commercial building. Both in ⅛″ scale.

Figure 68.   A ¼″-scale model based on the Culpeper building drawings in Figure 67.

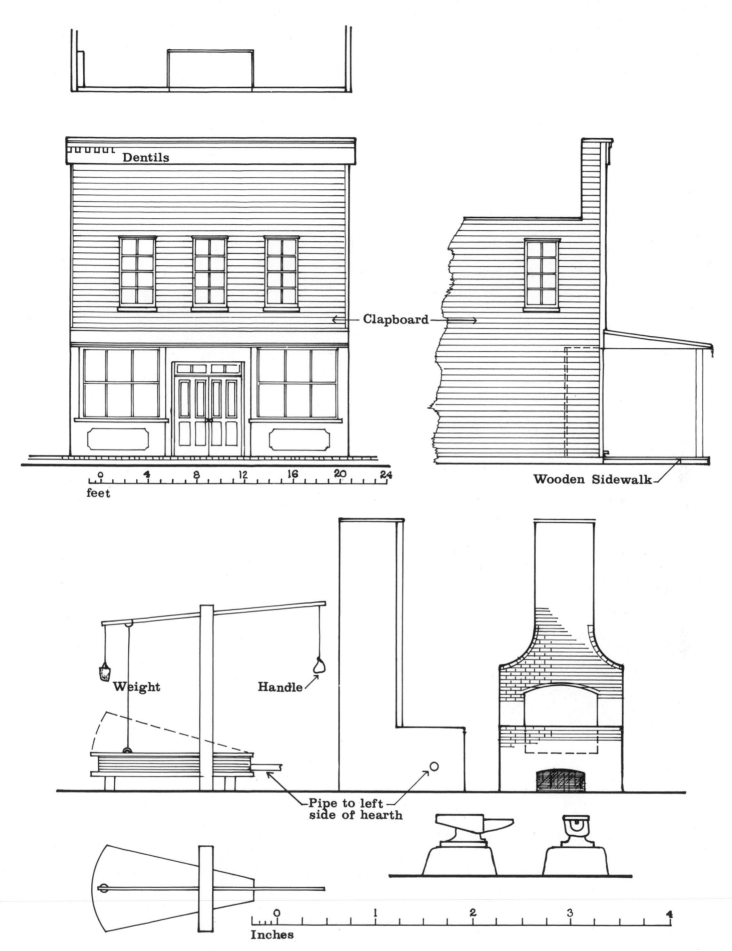

Figure 69. Above: A ⅛″-scale drawing of a general store with false front, from the Chattanooga area. *Below:* Details for a blacksmith shop, ¼″ scale.

Figure 70.   Above: ¼"-scale model based on drawing of general store in Figure 69. *Below:* Model of an old blacksmith shop.

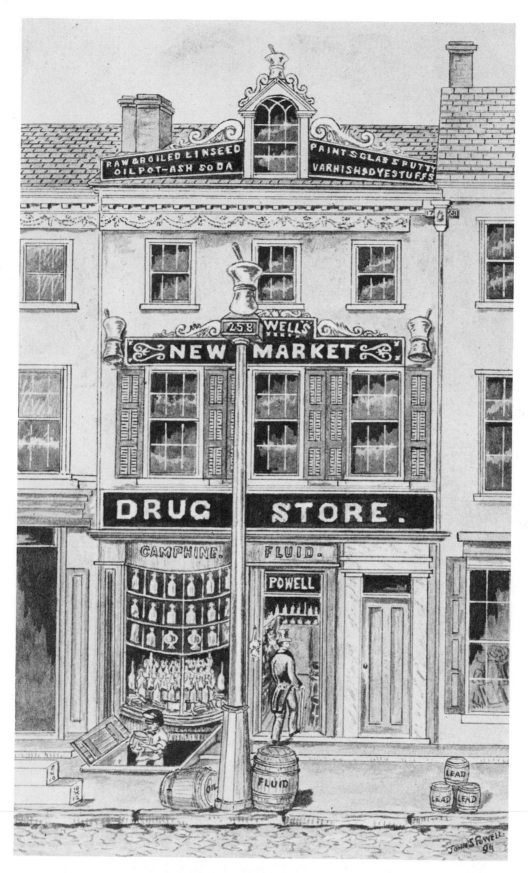

Figure 71. An 1860 drug and paint store in Philadelphia. From an old original watercolor (same size) by John Powell.

Figure 72. The Richmond & Petersburg Railroad bridge across the James River at Richmond. The Capitol Building is at upper right. See Chapter II, Figure 23, for remains at the end of the war.

Figure 73. From an old lithograph, the Cheat River Viaduct. Circa 1850.

CHAPTER V
Railroad Bridges

SEVERAL RAILROAD BRIDGES are illustrated in this chapter. Some of the Baltimore & Ohio's spans on their main stem, mentioned in Chapter I in connection with their destruction and rebuilding, are shown, as well as other bridges rebuilt as a result of the war.

A Pennsylvania Railroad bridge is illustrated to show how the rails were laid on stringers over the ties (Figure 78).

Figure 74.   The B & O's bridge across the Monongahela River at Fairmont, Virginia. Designed by Albert Fink, it was 650 feet long and 39 feet above water. Destroyed during the war, rebuilt 1863.

91

The old plans reproduced here are for more elaborate bridges than a small layout might require, but the ideas are there for one's own adaptation. The single-track covered bridge in Figures 79 and 80 would serve most needs. Note that there was no siding on these Southern railroad bridges; siding was more often seen in the North.

Figure 75. A typical view of a destroyed span, over the North Ana River north of Richmond.

Figure 76. Rebuilt bridge of the Manassas Gap Railroad, after the second battle of Bull Run.

Figure 77. Another view of the rebuilt Manassas Gap Railroad bridge.

Figure 78. A wooden bridge on the Pennsylvania Railroad showing construction with rails laid on stringers. The bridge is No. 12 over the Little Juniata River. The engine is the *Clarion*.

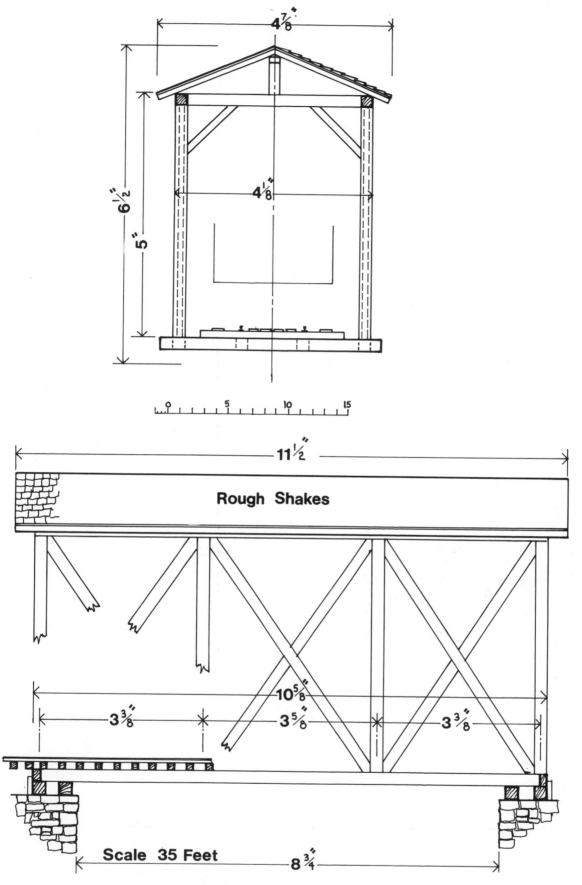

Figure 79a. A ⅛″-scale drawing of a railroad bridge of the 1860s, based on a Wilbur Kurtz sketch. (At night it was open, having no siding.)

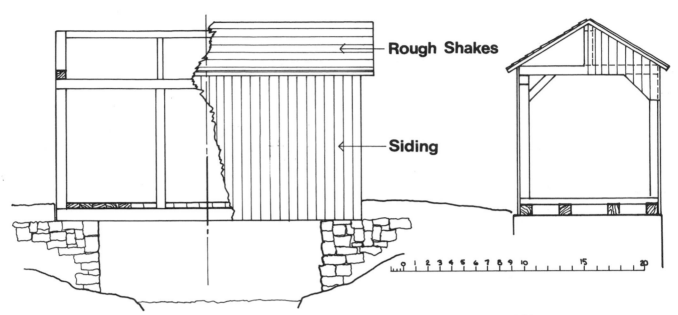

Figure 79b. A ⅛″-scale drawing of a wooden covered road bridge of the 1860s.

Figure 80. A ¼″-scale model of the railroad bridge in Figure 79b.

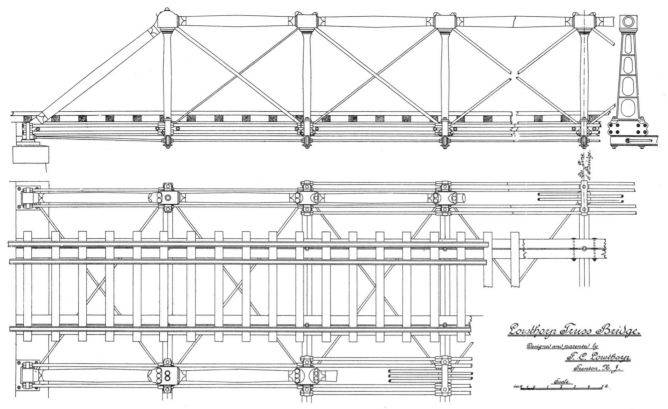

Figure 81. An old drawing of a Lowthorp bridge of the 1850s.

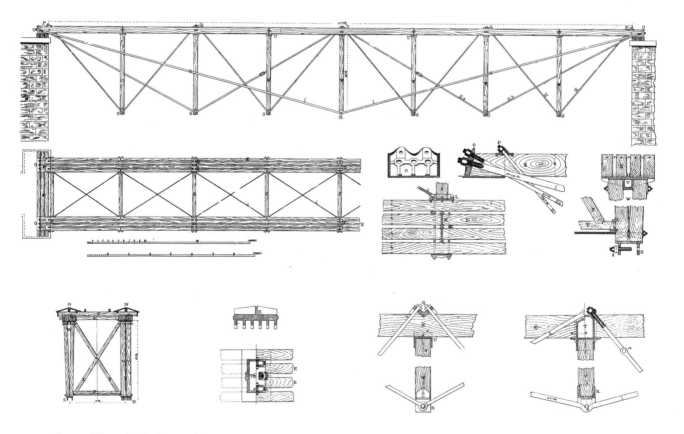

Figure 82. A Fink combination bridge—elevation, plan, and details (1850s).

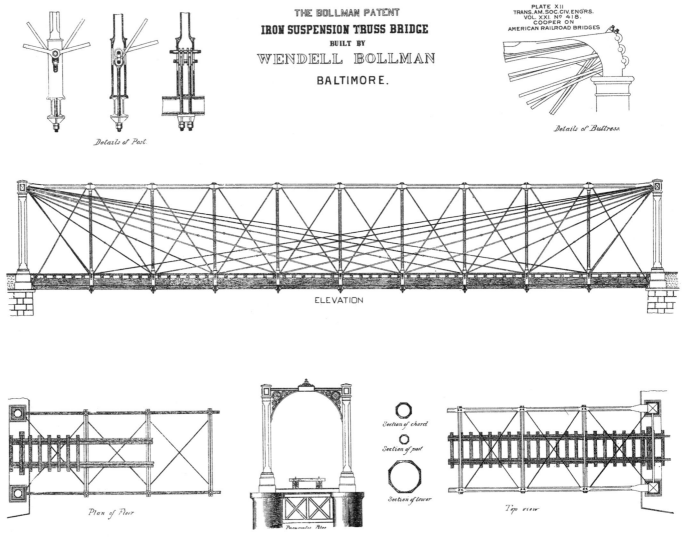

Figure 83.   Elevations and plans of a Bollman bridge, 1852.

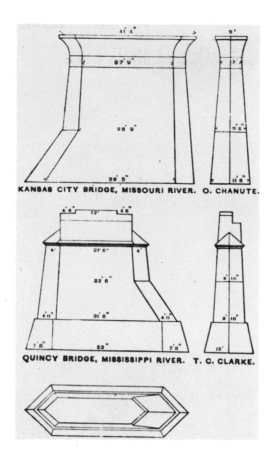

KANSAS CITY BRIDGE, MISSOURI RIVER. O. CHANUTE.

QUINCY BRIDGE, MISSISSIPPI RIVER. T. C. CLARKE.

OHIO RIVER BRIDGE, LOUISVILLE, KY. ALBERT FINK.

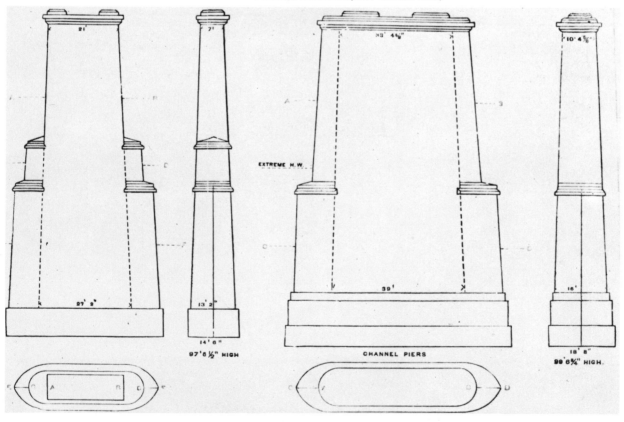

Figure 84. Various types of bridge piers of the 1850s.

Figure 85. One of the Newcastle-built locomotives acquired from the Philadelphia, Wilmington & Baltimore Railroad, probably the *Maryland.*

CHAPTER VI
United States Military Railroads & Locomotives

ERMAN HAUPT was the prime mover in organizing the United States Military Railroad. On April 27, 1862, he applied for a position as aide de camp on the staff of General McDowell, whom he had known at West Point. His first important work after arriving in Washington was rebuilding the Richmond, Fredericksburg and Potomac Railroad from Aquia Creek south of Alexandria to Fredericksburg, thus making it the first section of the United States Military Railroad. The wharf, all railroad bridges, and track had been destroyed, but Haupt had the road open by May 13, 1862. This was but a small hint of his ability to evaluate a situation and promptly take whatever corrective measures were necessary. On May 28, he was appointed a colonel, which he remained until after the second Battle of Bull Run, when he became a brigadier general.

Haupt was the righthand man of Colonel D. C. McCallum, General Manager of the U.S. Military Railroads, and what follows is an excerpt from Colonel McCallum's report of 1866, which is "must" reading for those interested in the many aspects of the first railroad war.

Report of Col. D. C. McCallum,
General Manager of the
U.S. Military Railroads, 1866.

Upon assuming the duties indicated in the above order (from Edwin M. Stanton Feb. 11, 1862) I found only one railroad in possession of the government—that from Washington to Alexandria, seven miles long, and in charge of Captain H. F. Morley, assistant quartermaster.

Previously, all passengers and freight had been transferred across the bridge [Long Bridge] by horse power.

In Alexandria the tracks had been laid through the city, to form a junction

Figure 86. No. 137, a Danforth, Cooke engine.

Figure 87. No. 89, the *Stuart Gwynn*, built by Taunton in 1863.

with the Orange and Alexandria railroad. The road was used regularly and continuously without interruption from this time forward until the close of the war, and on the 7th day of August, 1865, was surrendered to the Alexandria, Washington and Georgetown R. R. Co.

The transportation from February 9, 1862, to August 7, 1865, three years, five months, and twenty-eight days, was as follows:

Number of engines run [trains] over the road for other than local construction purposes . . . 8,983. Number of loaded cars . . . 30,457. Number of empty cars . . . 20,699. Total number of cars . . . 51,156.

In March, 1862, Major General McClellan instructed me to have a line examined for a railroad from Winchester, the terminus of the Harper's Ferry and Winchester railroad, to Strasburg, a station on the Manassas Gap railroad in the Shenandoah valley, and to make an estimate of the cost. This was completed in April but the railroad was not built.

March 14, 1862, General McClellan instructed me to have five locomotives and eighty cars loaded upon vessels in the harbor of Baltimore, and held subject to his orders with a view to using them in his contemplated peninsular campaign.

They were purchased from northern railroad companies, loaded as directed and remained on the vessels until early May, when they were sent to White House, Virginia and placed upon the Richmond and York River railroad.

Another engine was added in June to the number, and all employed in transporting supplies between White House and the front, which toward the close of June, was twenty miles from White House and four miles from Richmond. Upon the withdrawal of the army of the Potomac to Harrison's Landing, June 28, all the rolling stock was destroyed or damaged, as far as practicable, to prevent it from falling into the hands of the enemy.

Near the close of March, 1862, the Orange and Alexandria railroad was opened to Manassas Junction, twenty-six miles from Alexandria, and in April to Warrenton Junction, thirty-nine miles. In August, after relaying six miles of track and bridging the Rappahannock river, the road was opened to Culpeper, sixty-one miles, which at the time was the main depot for supplies of the army of Virginia. A few trains were run to the Rapidan river, eighty miles. Upon the retreat of General Pope, in the last days of August the road was entirely abandoned, with the loss of seven locomotives and two hundred and ninety-five cars. In November it was reopened for a few days to Bealton, forty-six miles, and to the town of Warrenton, to supply the army of the Potomac on its march from Antietam to Fredericksburg.

The Manassas Gap railroad was opened early in April, 1862, to Strasburg, sixty-one miles from Manassas and eighty-seven miles from Alexandria. It was operated only a very short time from Strasburg, but continued in use to Front Royal fifty-one miles from Manassas, through May and part of June, when it was abandoned.

In November, 1862, trains were run over it to Front Royal for a few days with supplies for General McClellan's army.

The Alexandria, Loudon & Hampshire railroad was opened in the spring of 1862 to Vienna, fifteen miles from Alexandria, and used for transporting supplies to the fortifications south of Washington, and the camps along its line. During the

Figure 88.   No. 150, built by New Jersey Locomotive & Machine Works in 1862.

first two weeks of September it was the principal line of supplies for the army of the Potomac, when encamped near Washington after the second battle of Bull Run, and previous to the Antietam campaign.

These four railroads comprise all that were operated as military lines from Alexandria to Washington. They were subsequently used, more or less, at various times . . . and continued to play an important part in the operations of the army of the Potomac.

In April, 1862, the Richmond, Fredericksburg and Potomac railroad was opened from Aquia Creek to Fredericksburg, fifteen miles, and operated to supply the forces stationed at Fredericksburg. The road was abandoned September 7, with the loss of one engine, fifty-seven cars, and a small quantity of material. On the 18th of November repairs were again commenced, and the road was opened on the 28th to Falmouth, opposite Fredericksburg, and was used to supply the army of the Potomac until June, 1863. A very large amount of work was required, not only to the railroad, but to the wharves at Aquia Creek, all of which had been burned when the line was abandoned by our forces. The limited accommodations for receiving and delivering freight and passengers at Aquia rendered an increase of wharf-room and tracks necessary, and a new wharf, afterwards named Yba Dam, was completed in February, one mile below the Aquia Creek wharf, and the necessary tracks laid from the main road to it. Vessels drawing ten and one half feet of water could land at the new wharf at low tide, while there was only eight and one half feet at high water at the old one. This improvement proved a valuable acquisition to the means of supplying the army.

Figure 89. No. 34, *Firefly,* built by Robert Norris & Son, 1862.

The road continued to be used without interruption until June, 1863, when it was abandoned with small loss of material; but the bridges, buildings and wharves were soon after burned by the enemy.

The eastern portion of the Norfolk and Petersburg railroad was taken in charge July 20, 1862, and the gauge at once changed from five feet to four feet eight and a half inches for forty-four miles. At Suffolk, twenty-three miles from Norfolk, this line crosses the Seaboard and Roanoke railroad running from Portsmouth opposite Norfolk. A connecting track was laid between the two roads in August, 1862, and these lines were afterwards operated together. In May, 1863, about fifteen miles of track were taken up on the Norfolk and Petersburg railroad west of Suffolk by order of Major General Dix, and about the same length on the Seaboard and Roanoke.

The two roads were afterwards operated to Suffolk, until the close of the war, for local military purposes and were not identified with any of the great military operations or campaigns.

In April, 1863, the Orange and Alexandria railroad was opened to Bealton, and used a few days to supply a force on the Rappahannock. The portion south of Bull Run was then abandoned, and on about the 15th of June the whole road outside the defenses of Washington was evacuated. July 18 repairs were recommenced and continued until the road was opened to Culpeper. Not having been much damaged by the enemy, the amount of work necessary to put it in running order was small. It was used until the first of October to supply the army of General Meade, after its return to Virginia from the Gettysburg campaign.

Early in October it was again abandoned south of Bull Run, and was thoroughly destroyed by the enemy from Manassas Junction nearly to Brandy station,

Figure 90. No. 76, the *General Haupt,* built by William Mason in 1863. It was later renamed the *General J. C. Robinson* (O. & A. R. R.).

about twenty-two miles. Repairs were commenced October 23 and the damaged road opened October 30 to Warrenton Junction, eleven miles, and to Culpeper, November 16, to which point it was operated during the winter, and until the final advance under Lieutenant General Grant, of the army of the Potomac, May 4, 1864, when it was abandoned beyond Burke's station, fourteen miles from Alexandria. Rappahannock river bridge, six hundred and twenty-five feet long, thirty-five feet high, was rebuilt in nineteen working hours. The army of the Potomac remained in winter quarters on the south side of the Rappahannock, and received all its supplies for men and animals during the winter and spring over this single track road.

The Manassas Gap railroad was reopened to White Plains, twenty-three miles from Manassas in August, 1863, and used for a few days to deliver supplies to General Meade's army on the march from Gettysburg to Culpeper.

On the 2nd day of July, 1863, military possession was taken of the Western Maryland railroad from Baltimore to Westminster, in Maryland thirty-six miles, which, from its position, had become the line of supply for the army of General Meade at Gettysburg. Sufficient locomotives, cars, fuel, supplies and men to operate it were brought from the military railroads of Virginia, the equipment belonging to the road itself being wholly inadequate. The road was restored to the

Figure 91. No. 133, built by Danforth, Cooke. Photographed at City Point.

owners July 7, the army having moved to the line of the Baltimore & Ohio railroad.

July 9, 1863 full military possession was taken of the railroad from Hanover Junction to Gettysburg, thirty miles, and it was operated as a military line until August 1, to remove wounded from the field of battle to distant hospitals. During military occupation, about 15,580 wounded men were transported over it. The equipment and men for this work were likewise furnished from the military railroads of Virginia.

During the rebel occupation of central Pennsylvania in June, all the bridges were destroyed by them on the Northern Central railroad between Hanover Junction and Harrisburg, and several miles of track torn up on the Cumberland Valley and Franklin railroads between Harrisburg and Hagerstown, Maryland. The Virginia military railroad construction corps rebuilt the bridges of the Northern Central railroad. The materials for the same were furnished from the government yard at Alexandria, Virginia. The railroad company afterwards returned an equal quantity of material, the lumber amounting to 150,000 feet, board measure. The same construction corps also relaid a portion of the damaged track of the Cumberland Valley and Franklin railroads.

As the war progressed the nature, capacity and the value of railroads was better understood on both sides, and more systematic and determined efforts were made by the enemy against the line used for transporting supplies to our armies. The destruction of track and bridges was greater each subsequent time the roads passed within their military lines and it became apparent that extraordinary preparations must be made to meet it.

Early in 1863 a small construction corps was formed, consisting of about three hundred men which was the beginning of an organization afterwards numbering in the east and west nearly 10,000. The design of the corps was to combine a body of skilled workmen in each department of railroad construction and repairs, under competent engineers, supplied with abundant materials, tools, mechanical appliances and transportation.

They were formed into divisions, gangs and squads in charge respectively of supervisors, foremen and sub-foremen, furnished with tents and field equipment. Storehouses were established at principal points with ample stock of tools and materials.

With the opening of the campaign in Virginia in May, 1864, under Lieutenant General Grant, the Alexandria railroad ceased to bear any important part. The Orange and Alexandria line was open to Rappahannock river, fifty miles, between September 28 and October 2, 1864 but at once abandoned back to Manassas. It was operated to that station until November 10, when it was abandoned back to Fairfax, sixteen miles from Alexandria.

It was operated for that distance until the close of the war, and on June 27, 1865 was surrendered to the board of public works of Virginia.

The Manassas Gap railroad was open from Manassas to Piedmont, thirty-four miles, between October the 3rd and 11th, and operated until October 27, 1864. Between that date and November 10, the rails were taken up between the above named stations and carried to Alexandria.

On the 9th of May, 1864, repairs were again commenced on the railroad at Aquia Creek and it was opened to Falmouth, fourteen miles, May 17.

Potomac Creek bridge, seven miles from Aquia, four hundred and fourteen feet long and eighty-two feet high was built, ready for trains to pass in forty working hours.

The road was operated until May 22, principally for removing the wounded of the battles at Spottsylvania Court House. On that day it was abandoned and not long afterwards used as a military line.

The Richmond and York River railroad was opened about the 1st of June from White House to Despatch, fourteen miles, and operated until June 10 when it was finally abandoned, the track taken up by order of Lieutenant Grant, and the materials removed to Alexandria.

Rolling stock for the Aquia Creek and York River railroads were sent from Alexandria on barges prepared with tracks for the purpose, and taken away in the same manner without loss or injury when the roads were abandoned.

Near the close of June, 1864, the City Point and Petersburg was occupied to Pitkin station, eight miles from City Point.

During the fall and winter of 1864 and 1865, eighteen miles of new railroad were built passing around to the south and southwest of the city of Petersburg, by which the armies of General Grant were principally supplied.

Figure 92. A ¼″-scale model of a Grant Locomotive Works 2-4-2 engine with an Orange & Alexandria Railroad coach.

The Richmond and Petersburg railroad was opened April 4, 1865 from Petersburg to the south bank of the James river, opposite Richmond, twenty-one miles, and was operated by this department until July 3, when it was turned over to the Virginia board of public works.

The Petersburg and Lynchburg railroad was repaired between April 4th and 11th, to Burkesville, sixty-two miles from City Point and used for a short time to supply the armies of General Meade and the paroled soldiers of General Lee's army. The gauge was originally five (5) feet, but not having proper rolling stock at hand, it was changed to four feet, eight and one half inches. It was operated as a military road until July 24, when it was turned over to the board of public works.

Shortly after the surrender of General Johnston's army, the Richmond and Danville railroad was opened to Danville, one hundred and forty miles, and operated for military purposes until July 4, 1865, when it also, was surrendered to the board of public works.

The Winchester and Potomac railroad was repaired from Harper's Ferry to Halltown, six miles, between August the 14th and 19th, 1864, to Stevenson, twenty-eight miles, between November 2nd and 24th, and was used to supply the army of General Sheridan, operating in the valley of Virginia. The iron used in the reconstruction of this line was principally taken from the Manassas Gap railroad. The bridges all were rebuilt. The road remained in charge of this department until January 20, 1866, when it was restored to the railroad Company.

The railroads in Virginia, Maryland, and Pennsylvania, used at any time

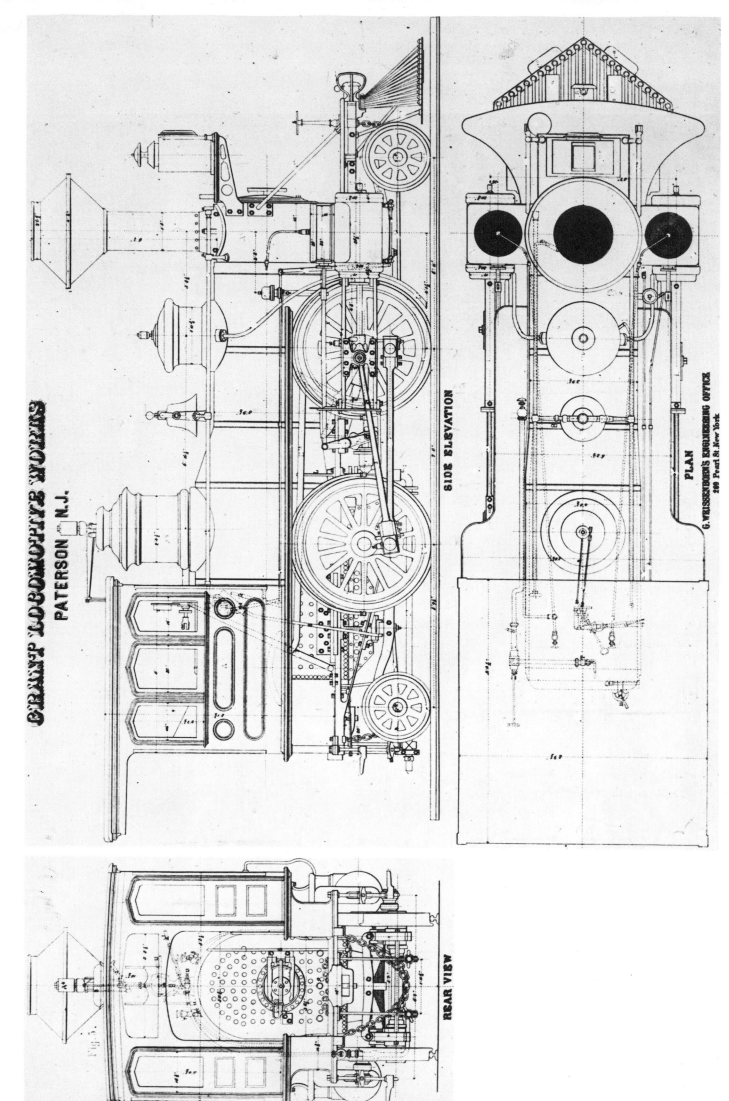

GRANT LOCOMOTIVE WORKS

PATERSON N.J.

SIDE ELEVATION

REAR VIEW

PLAN

G. WEISSENBORN'S ENGINEERING OFFICE
269 Pearl St. New York

Figure 93. Elevation and plan of the Grant Locomotive from which the model in Figure 92 was made.

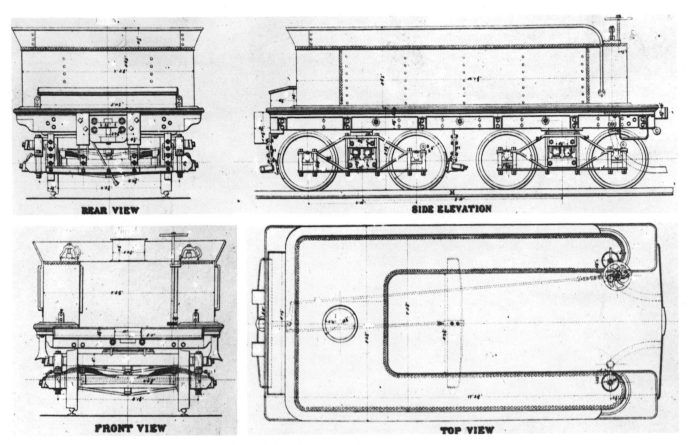

Figure 94. Elevations and plan of the Grant tender.

during the war as military lines, the terminal stations on each while so used, and the number of miles operated, were as follows:

Alexandria & Washington	Alexandria–Washington	7 miles
Alexandria, Loudon & Hampshire	Alexandria–Vienna	15 miles
Orange & Alexandria	Alexandria–Mitchell's	68 miles
Warrenton Branch	Warrenton Jct.–Warrenton	9 miles
Manassas Gap	Manassas–Strasburg	62 miles
Richmond, Fredericksburg & Potomac	Aquia Creek–Fredericksburg	15 miles
Richmond & York River	White House–Fair Oaks	20 miles
Richmond & Petersburg	Manchester–Petersburg	22 miles
Clover Hill Branch	Clover Hill–Coal Mines	18 miles
Richmond & Danville	Manchester–Danville	140 miles
South Side	City Point–Burkesville	62 miles
Army Line & Branches	Pitkin, etc. Humphrey, etc.	18 miles
Norfolk & Petersburg	Norfolk–Blackwater	44 miles
Seaboard & Roanoke	Portsmouth–Suffolk	17 miles
Winchester & Potomac	Harper's Ferry–Stevenson	28 miles
Western Maryland	Baltimore–Westminster	36 miles
Hanover Br. & Gettysburg	Hanover Jct.–Gettysburg	30 miles
	Total:	611 miles

The operations in Western Tennessee and Kentucky, and in north Mississippi, were distinct and separate from those at Nashville and although under the control of the general superintendent at the latter point, they required and received very little attention as compared with the lines leading to the front.

The Nashville and Chattanooga railroad, 151 miles, was the great main line over which passed all the supplies for the armies of the Cumberland, the Ohio, and the Tennessee, through the campaigns which terminated with the occupation of Atlanta. Over this single line of railroad the provisions, clothing, and camp equipage for the men, forage for animals, arms, ammunition, and ordnance stores, re-enforcements, and all the varied miscellaneous supplies required for a great army engaged in an active campaign, were sent to the front; and by it were returned the sick, wounded, disabled and discharged soldiers, refugees and freed men, captured prisoners, and materials deemed advisable to send to the rear.

Portions of the road had been in use for military purposes since April, 1862, but I have not in my possession any data of the operations of this or any other military line of the southwest prior to February, 1864.

About 115 miles of track were re-laid with new iron, cross-ties and ballast from February, 1864 to the close of the war. Sidings were put in at intervals, to be not more than eight miles apart, each capable of holding five to eight long freight trains, and telegraph stations were established at most of them. In all, nineteen miles of new sidings were added to the road and forty-five new water tanks were erected.

During the spring and summer of 1864, a few occasional guerrilla raids were made upon it, but they caused little damage to property or detention to transportation. About September 1, 1864, the rebel General Wheeler destroyed seven miles of the road between Nashville and Murfreesboro. In December, General Hood destroyed seven and three-fourth miles of track and five hundred and thirty feet of bridges between the same stations. In both cases the road was promptly repaired and trains running in a few days. The road was turned over to the company September 15, 1865.

The next railroad in importance for military purposes was the Western and Atlantic, from Chattanooga to Atlanta, 136 miles. It was opened to Ringgold, Georgia, 21 miles from Chattanooga in March, 1864. Early in May the work of reconstruction was commenced south from Ringgold and kept pace with the movements of Sherman's army. The line was opened through to Atlanta in August 1864, immediately after the evacuation of the town by the rebel army. In the reconstruction of this road 22½ miles of track and 4,081 lineal feet of bridges were rebuilt.

The most important single structure was Chattahoochie bridge, 780 feet long and 92 feet high, which was completed by the construction corps in four and a half days. While occupied as a military road this was more infested by guerrillas than any other during the war. Every device possible to apply was used to throw trains off the track and though occasionally successful, the preparations to guard against such attempts were so complete that few of them caused loss of life or more than a few hours detention.

Early in October, 1864, General Hood passed around General Sherman's army and fell upon the railroad at several points in its rear. He destroyed 35½ miles of track and 455 lineal feet of bridges, but in thirteen days after he left the line it was repaired and trains were run over its entire length.

Figure 95. The Louisville engine house and facilities at Nashville with U. S. Military R. R. engines. *Left to right:* Locomotives No. 131 and 132. *Facing, next to shed:* No. 83.

Twenty-five miles of track and 230 feet of bridges, in one stretch, between Tunnel Hill and Resaca were constructed in seven and a half days. This was accomplished by working from each end of the break and at the same time working both ways from Dalton which was reached by trains with material by way of Cleveland after relaying one and a half miles of track.

When General Sherman commenced his march to Savannah in November, the road between Atlanta and Dalton, 100 miles, was abandoned, the track from Atlanta to Etowah river, 46 miles, was torn up and destroyed, and from Resaca to Dalton, 16 miles, the rails were taken up and carried to Chattanooga.

By order of Major General Thomas the road from Dalton to Atlanta was reconstructed and between May 10 and July 4, 1865, sixty-six miles of track were laid, 36 miles repaired and 3,553 lineal feet of bridges rebuilt.

On the 25th day of September, 1865, it was turned over to the State of Georgia, to whom it originally belonged.

The East Tennessee and Georgia railroad, from Chattanooga to Knoxville, 112 miles, was opened through in May, 1864, upon completion of Tennessee River bridge at Loudon. It had been used for three months previous by trans-shipping stores and passengers across the river in flat-boats. It was operated with great regularity during the entire military occupation of that region, except in August and September, 1864 when General Wheeler tore up 25 miles of track. It was speedily repaired and not molested afterwards.

The Dalton branch from Cleveland to Dalton, 27 miles, was operated in connection with the main line, and was of great service on several occasions. On the 28th day of August, 1865, the road and branch were restored to the company.

The East Tennessee and Virginia railroad, from Knoxville to Bristol was used and abandoned for short distances near Knoxville during 1864. The furthest point reached during the year was at Bull's Gap, 56 miles from Knoxville. By orders of Major General Thomas repairs were commenced near Knoxville March 4, 1865, and the road opened to Carter's station, 110 miles, April 23. Between those dates 12 miles of track were rebuilt, ninety-four miles repaired and 4,400 lineal feet of bridges reconstructed. It was turned over to the company August 28, 1865.

The Nashville, Decatur and Stevenson line is formed of the Nashville and Decatur railroad, 120 miles from Nashville, south to Decatur, on Tennessee river together with the eastern portion of the Memphis and Charleston railroad, from Decatur to Stevenson, 80 miles. Stevenson is at the junction of the latter railroad and the Nashville and Chattanooga, being 113 miles distant from Nashville.

Although the distance via Decatur is 87 miles greater than by direct road, such was the pressure for transportation it was necessary to send return trains by that route from the front until the capacity of the Nashville and Chattanooga line was sufficiently increased to accommodate the business. In June, 1864, all through trains were transferred to the main line.

The Nashville, Decatur and Stevenson line was used for local purposes during the summer of 1864. About the first of September General Wheeler tore up several miles of the track between Nashville and Columbia, and late in September General Forrest destroyed several bridges and tore up a portion of the track between Athens and Pulaski. The whole length of the track destroyed in the two raids was 29½ miles. That between Nashville and Columbia was at once repaired but between Pulaski and Athens it was not rebuilt until February, 1865. During Hood's Nashville campaign, in November and December, 1864, all the bridges then standing between Nashville and Decatur were destroyed, with six miles of track. The work of reconstruction was commenced on December 19, three days after the battle of Nashville, and completed to Pulaski, February 10, 1865. In addition to relaying the track, 7,055 lineal feet of bridges were built, consuming 1,045,675 feet of timber (board measure).

Near the close of February, and again in March, most of the bridges were swept away by extraordinary floods, and were rebuilt, some of them twice, and many of them three times; and they were finally replaced by permanent truss bridges.

The road from Stevenson to Decatur was restored to the company September 12 and between Nashville and Decatur, September 15, 1865. At the beginning of the war, the Nashville and Northwestern had been completed to Kingston Springs, 25 miles from Nashville, and some of the work had been done upon it thence to Tennessee River.

On the 17th day of February, 1864, the supervision of the work of construction was placed in my charge by order of Major General Grant. The road was connected through between Nashville and Tennessee River on the 10th day of May, 1864. On the 9th of August it was turned over to this department to be operated as a military line, by an order of Major General Sherman, issued by the authority of the President of the United States. At the terminus on Tennessee river, named Johnsonville, extensive arrangements were made to receive and transfer freight from steamboats to cars. Ample buildings and platforms were erected and powerful handling machinery introduced. During the months of August, September and October, the season of low water in Cumberland river, large quantities of supplies for the army were received and shipped over the road. It was very much exposed to attacks from guerrillas who at times inflicted considerable damage, and interfered with its operation. On the 4th of November, General Forrest planted batteries on the west bank of Tennessee river, and succeeded in destroying all the valuable buildings of Johnsonville with their contents. On the 30th of November the road was entirely abandoned, and the movable property on it taken to Nashville. During General Hood's occupation of the country, from December 1 to 16, all the bridges were destroyed. Repairs were commenced January 2 and the road completed through February 13, 2,200 lineal feet of bridges were rebuilt. In February, March and April most of these bridges were swept away by floods, and rebuilt, some of them three times. In May and June, 1865, all were replaced by permanent truss bridges.

On the 1st of September, 1865, the road was turned over to the railroad company.

The Nashville and Clarksville line was formed of the Edgefield and Kentucky railroad, 47 miles from Nashville, and 15 miles of the Memphis, Clarksville and Louisville railroad. It was repaired and opened in August, 1864, by order of Major General Sherman, in order to have another railroad communication with water navigable in summer, to aid in supplying the Nashville depot.

Important bridges were destroyed by floods at various times and rebuilt until in April, 1865, when its use as a military road was abandoned except on the 28 miles nearest Nashville. It was turned over to the company September 23, 1865.

After the war closed the railroads leading south from Nashville were kept in active operations for some months, transporting paroled prisoners to their homes, and returning those who had been confined in camps north of the Ohio river, together with the movement of Union troops to be mustered out or take up new positions in Tennessee and Georgia.

In 1862 several lines and many miles of railroad were operated for military purposes from Memphis, Tennessee and Columbus, Kentucky but no reports or statements of their business have been in my hands.

At Columbus, Kentucky, I found the Mobile and Ohio railroad open to Union City, 26 miles. It was abandoned about the first of May, 1864 at the time of Forrest's raid upon Union City, and not afterwards used, except in the immediate vicinity of Columbus until May, 1865. It was reopened to Union City, 35 miles May 31; and restored to the company August 25, 1865.

The Memphis and Little Rock railroad, between Devil's Bluff and Little Rock, 49 miles, was the only line operated in Arkansas. It did not come under my control until May 1, 1865. It was then in very bad condition in consequence of the nature of the soil and neglect or want of skill in keeping up the necessary repairs. It was operated as a military line until November 1, 1865, when it was restored to the company.

Statement of railroads operated in Tennessee, Georgia, Mississippi, Kentucky and Arkansas:

Name of Line	Greatest No. of Miles Operated	Turned over to Owners
Nashville & Chattanooga	151	Sept. 15, 1865
Nashville, Decatur & Stevenson	200	Sept. 15, 1865
Nashville & Northwestern	78	Sept. 1, 1865
Nashville & Clarksville	62	Sept. 23, 1865
Shelbyville Branch	9	Sept. 15, 1865
McMinnville & Manchester	35	
Mount Pleasant Branch	12	Sept. 15, 1865
Chattanooga & Knoxville	112	Aug. 28, 1865
Cleveland & Dalton	27	Aug. 28, 1865
Knoxville & Bristol	110	Aug. 28, 1865
Rogersville & Jefferson	12	
Chattanooga & Atlanta	136	Sept. 28, 1865
Rome Branch	17	
Atlanta & Macon	11	
Memphis & Charleston	75	Sept. 12, 1865
Mississippi Central	68	Sept. 12, 1865
Mobile & Ohio	15	Aug. 25, 1865
Memphis & Little Rock	49	Nov. 1, 1865
Louisville City	2	

Total: 1201 miles

Under orders received from Major General McClellan, four locomotives and one hundred freight cars were sent to Major General Burnside at Newbern, North Carolina, in the months of June and July, 1862. On the passage two locomotives were lost with the vessel off Cape Hatteras, and two others were afterwards sent to replace them. One engine proving unserviceable was subsequently returned to Alexandria, Virginia, leaving three locomotives and one hundred cars in service. The road was worked under orders and by officers appointed by the general commanding the department, and did not come under my jurisdiction. I am therefore unable to give any account of its operation.

When it was ascertained to what point of the coast General Sherman was directing his march from Atlanta, preparations were at once made to furnish him with railroad facilities. A portion of the construction corps from the division of the Mississippi, that had rebuilt the railroads during the Atlanta campaign, were ordered in December, 1864, to proceed to Baltimore via railroad from Nashville and embark for Savannah. Upon reaching Hilton Head, information was received that General Sherman would not use the railroads near Savannah and orders were given to proceed to Newbern, North Carolina, and open the railroad to Goldsboro. Eleven miles of the Savannah and Gulf railroad were opened and operated with rolling stock captured at Savannah for local military purposes and to supply citizens of the town with fuel. The tracks and buildings of the Georgia

Figure 96. To the right of Figure 95 is the train shed of the Nashville station, which in turn is still farther to the right.

Central railroad within the city limits were also used. Five serviceable and nine unserviceable locomotives, and two hundred and thirteen cars, about one half of them damaged and unfit for service, were captured at Savannah.

On the 20th day of June, 1865, all the railroad property was restored to the original owners by order of the department commander.

A detachment of the Virginia construction corps was sent to North Carolina by order of General Grant and landed at Newbern January 30, 1865. The railroad at that time was in charge of the depot quartermaster at Newbern, and was in operation between Morehead City and Batchelor's Creek, forty-four miles. This construction force at once commenced rebuilding the bridge over that stream. On the 6th day of February the detachment sent from the military division of the Mississippi landed at Morehead City and relieved the force from Virginia, which returned to City Point.

The railroad was required as fast as the army advanced, and was opened to Goldsboro, ninety-five miles, March 25, the day following the arrival of General Sherman and his army from Savannah.

To provide another line of supplies the railroad from Wilmington to Goldsboro, eighty-five miles, was repaired and opened through April 4.

On the 10th of April movements were resumed toward the interior and the railroad was opened April 19 to Raleigh, forty-eight miles from Goldsboro. It was

Figure 97. Two ¼″-scale models of U. M. R. R. 4-4-0 locomotives showing variations in lettering.

opened soon after to Hillsboro, and used until the parole of General Johnston's army was completed, when it was given up west of Raleigh.

The total length of railroads opened and used in this department was as follows:

Name of Line	Terminal Stations	Miles	Returned to Company
Atlantic & North Carolina	Morehead City–Goldsboro	95	Oct. 25, 1865
Wilmington & Weldon	Wilmington–Goldsboro	85	Aug. 27, 1865
North Carolina	Goldsboro–Hillsboro	88	Oct. 22, 1865
Raleigh & Gaston	Raleigh–Cedar Creek	25	May 3, 1865

U. S. Military Railroads (East)

ENGINES BUILT BEFORE 1863

Year	Number	Name	Builder	Drivers	Originally Acquired from
1840	93	Romulus	Norris	48″	
1843	19	Panther	Hinkley & Drury	36″	Boston & Worcester R. R.
1844	5	Brattleboro	Hinkley & Drury	60″	Fitchburg R. R.
1844	6	Lexington	Hinkley & Drury	60″	Fitchburg R. R.
1846	17	Job Terry	Hinkley & Drury	60″	Old Colony & Fall River R. R.
1846	30	Washington	Baldwin	46″	?
1846	31	Indiana	Baldwin	46″	?
1848	1	Ontario	Hinkley & Drury	46″	Fitchburg R. R.
1848	2	Lincoln	Hinkley & Drury	54″	Fitchburg R. R.
1848	20	Contest	Hinkley & Drury	69″	Nashua & Lowell R. R.
1848	21	Victor	Hinkley & Drury	69″	Nashua & Lowell R. R.
1849	16	Sentinel	Seth Wilmarth	50″	Old Colony & Fall River R. R. was "Dorchester"
1850	26	A. A. Bunting	Amoskeag	60″	Concord R. R. was "Rob Roy"
1851	25	Fairfax	Smith & Perkins	60″	Orange & Alexandria R. R.
1852	7	Warrior	Rogers, K. & G.	66″	C. R. R. New Jersey
1853	8	Wyandank	Baldwin	48″	Long Island R. R. was "Thornton"
?	23	Senator	Amoskeag	60″	Concord R. R.
1853	24	Epping	Souther	66″	?
1853	82	Maryland	Newcastle	56″	?
1853	136	(B & O 136)	Winans	43″	?
1854	3	Hoosac	Souther	56″	Fitchburg R. R.
1854	4	Champion	Souther	56″	Fitchburg R. R.
1855	51	Blue Bird	Baldwin	48″	Phila. & Reading R. R.
1863	81	Humming Bird	Baldwin	56″	Phila. & Reading R. R.
1856	25	E. J. M. Hale	Amoskeag	60″	?
1856	27	Exeter	Hinkley & Drury	54″	Boston & Maine R. R.
1856	28	Dover	Hinkley & Drury	54″	Boston & Maine R. R.
1856	94	Rapidan	Va. Loco & Car Wks.	50″	?
1859	18	Speedwell	Lawrence Mach. Shop	54″	?

The following locomotives were built in 1862 and 1863, except those with "?"

Year	Number	Name	Builder	Drivers	
1863	9	J. H. Devereux	N. J. Loco & Mach. Co.	60″	
?	10	Scout	N. J. Loco & Mach. Co.	60″	
?	11	Waterford	N. J. Loco & Mach. Co.	60″	
?	12	No. 2	N. J. Loco & Mach. Co.	60″	
?	13	No. 1	N. J. Loco & Mach. Co.	?	
?	14	Vidette	?	69″	
?	15	Capt. Ferguson	?	69″	
?	22	Monitor	Souther	56″	
1862	32	Romeo	R. Norris & Sons.	48″	
1862	33	Spark	R. Norris & Sons.	?	
1862	34	Firefly	R. Norris & Sons.	56″	
1862	35	Hero	R. Norris & Sons.	54″	

1862	36	Edwin M. Stanton	R. Norris & Sons.	48″	
1862	37	Samson	Baldwin	48″	
1862	38	Union	Baldwin	50″	
1862	39	Vulcan	Baldwin	60″	
1862	40	G. A. Parker	Baldwin	60″	
1862	41	Osceola	Rogers	54″	
1862	42	President	Rogers	54″	
1862	43	Gen'l McClellan	N. J. Loco & Mach. Co.	60″	
1862	44	Col. McCallum	N. J. Loco & Mach. Co.	60″	
1862	45	Red Bird	N. J. Loco & Mach. Co.	60″	
1862	46	Government	N. J. Loco & Mach. Co.	60″	
1862	47	Secretary	Taunton	60″	
1862	48	Chief	Taunton	60″	
1862	49	W. H. Whiton	Mason	60″	
1862	50	E. L. Wentz	Mason	60″	
1862	52	F. Leach	N. J. L. & M. Co.	56″	
1862	54	Robeson	R. Norris & Son	56″	
1862	55	W. H. Whiton	R. Norris & Son	56″	different from No. 49
1862	56	Madison	R. Norris & Son	56″	
1862	57	Monroe	R. Norris & Son	56″	
1862	58	Jefferson	R. Norris & Son	56″	
1862	59	Washington	R. Norris & Son	56″	
1862	60	Gen'l Halleck	Rogers L. & M. Co.	56″	
1862	61	Eagle	N. J. L. & M. Co.	60″	
1862	62	J. O. D. Lilly	Baldwin	56″	
1862	63	Reindeer	R. Norris & Son	60″	
1862	64	Manfred	R. Norris & Son	56″	
1862	65	May Queen	R. Norris & Son	56″	
1862	66	Pickwick	R. Norris & Son	56″	
1862	67	Hiawatha	R. Norris & Son	56″	
1862	68	Lion	N. J. L. & M. Co.	56″	
1862	69	Tiger	N. J. L. & M. Co.	56″	
1862	70	Zebra	N. J. L. & M. Co.	56″	
1862	71	C. H. Vibard	Baldwin	56″	
1862	72	Gen'l Dix	Baldwin	60″	
1862	73	Fury	Rogers L. & M. Co.	54″	
1863	74	Buffalo	Rogers L. & M. Co.	54″	
1862	75	H. L. Robinson	Mason	60″	
1863	76	Gen'l Haupt	Mason	60″	
1863	77	Gen'l Burnside	Mason	60″	
1863	78	Gen'l Sickles	Mason	60″	
1863	79	E. Corning	Taunton	60″	
1863	80	Grapeshot	Taunton	60″	
1863	83	Gov. Nye	R. Norris & Son	60″	
1863	84	Gen'l Meigs	R. Norris & Son	60″	
1863	85	Col. A. Beckwith	R. Norris & Son	60″	
1863	86	C. Minot	N. J. L. & M. Co.	60″	
1863	87	Commodore	N. J. L. & M. Co.	60″	
1863	88	Gen'l Couch	Taunton	60″	
1863	89	Stuart Gwynn	Taunton	60″	
1863	90	W. W. Wright	Rogers L. & M. Co.	60″	

CHAPTER VII
Northern Locomotives

THE NORTHERN RAILROADS most affected by the Civil War, other than the Baltimore & Ohio, were the Northern Central, the Cumberland Valley, the Philadelphia, Wilmington & Baltimore, and the Pennsylvania. The first three were closely affiliated with the Pennsylvania. Military movements of men and equipment via the Pennsylvania were transferred to the Northern Central at Harrisburg for shipment to Baltimore. At Philadelphia the Philadelphia, Wilmington & Baltimore provided the eastern route for shipments to the latter city. The Cumberland Valley also carried Baltimore-bound traffic to Hagerstown, where it was transhipped to the Baltimore & Ohio.

Ten of the northern locomotives illustrated here are Pennsylvania and a few are P. W. & B. and C. V. engines. A number of contemporary lithographs are reproduced as well to show other types of typical motive power. Where possible the drawings are to ¼″ scale as a guide for dimensions and they are noted as such in the captions. Some tenders by several locomotive builders are also included.

The motive power of the Philadelphia, Wilmington & Baltimore was not adequate to meet government requirements in 1861. At the close of the fiscal year October 31, 1861, the company owned thirty-two locomotive engines, twenty-four of which were located on the Philadelphia, Wilmington & Baltimore Railroad and eight on the New Castle and Wilmington, the New Castle and Frenchtown, the Delaware, Eastern Shore and Junction, and the Breakwater railroads. The first twenty-four were as follows:

Name of Engine	Builder	When Placed in Service
America	New Castle Mfg. Co.	1854
Edward Austin	Baldwin & Co.	1861
Baltimore	Company (P. W. & Bo.)	No record
Brandywine	Baldwin & Co.	1848
Christiana	Baldwin & Co.	1837
Cincinnati	New Castle Mfg. Co.	1853
Constitution	New Castle Mfg. Co.	1854
Henry Clay	Taunton Mfg. Co.	1858
Empire	Company	1851
J. M. Forbes	Baldwin & Co.	1861
Gunpowder	Company	1853
Goliah	New Castle Mfg. Co.	1853
Magnolia	Company	1854
Maryland	New Castle Mfg. Co.	1853

Mississippi	New Castle Mfg. Co.	1848
C. W. Morris	New Castle Mfg. Co.	1854
Pennsylvania	New Castle Mfg. Co.	1853
Samson	New Castle Mfg. Co.	1853
William Sturgis	Taunton Mfg. Co.	1860
John E. Thayer	Baldwin & Co.	1859
Virginia	New Castle Mfg. Co.	1854
Wilmington	New Castle Mfg. Co.	1852
George Washington	Baldwin & Co.	1859
Daniel Webster	Taunton Mfg. Co.	1858

These engines were all in service with the exception of the *Christiana*. The other eight machines were as follows:

Victory	New Castle Mfg. Co.	1847
Boston	New Castle Mfg. Co.	1848
Delaware	New Castle Mfg. Co.	1851
Philadelphia	New Castle Mfg. Co.	1852
New Castle	New Castle Mfg. Co.	1852
William Penn	New Castle Mfg. Co.	1855
Thomas Clayton	New Castle Mfg. Co.	1857
Princess Anne	New Castle Mfg. Co.	1858

However, the company did a wonderful amount of work with the available power and immediately arranged to increase it. Before the war closed the company was prepared to meet all demands upon it.

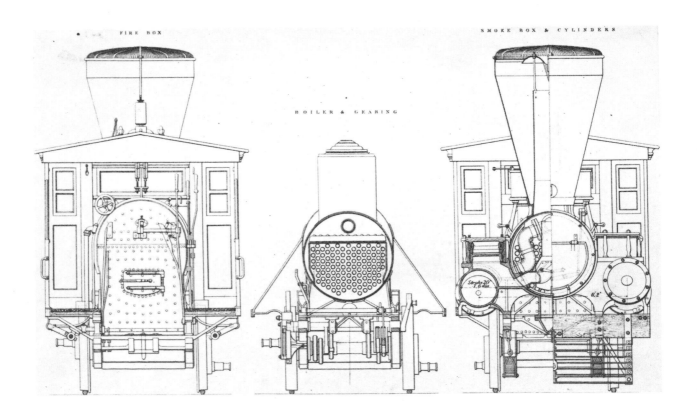

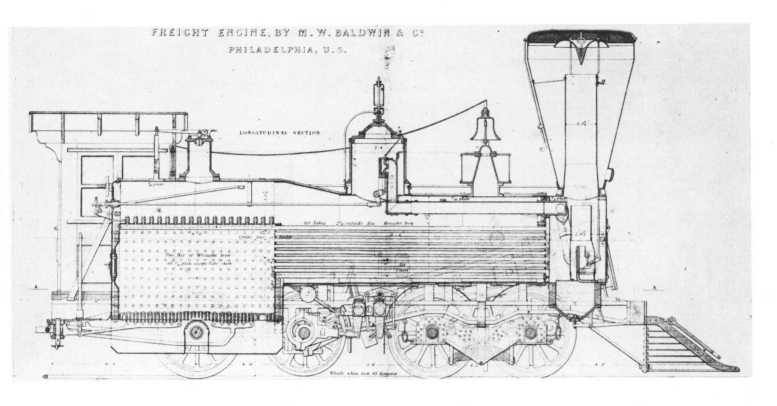

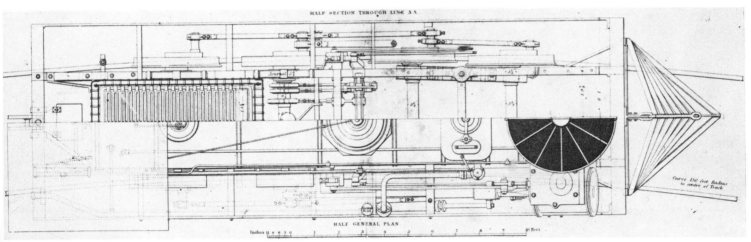

Figure 98. Opposite and this page: Elevations and plan of a Baldwin flexible-beam truck engine (circa 1848) as built for the Pennsylvania and B & O railroads.

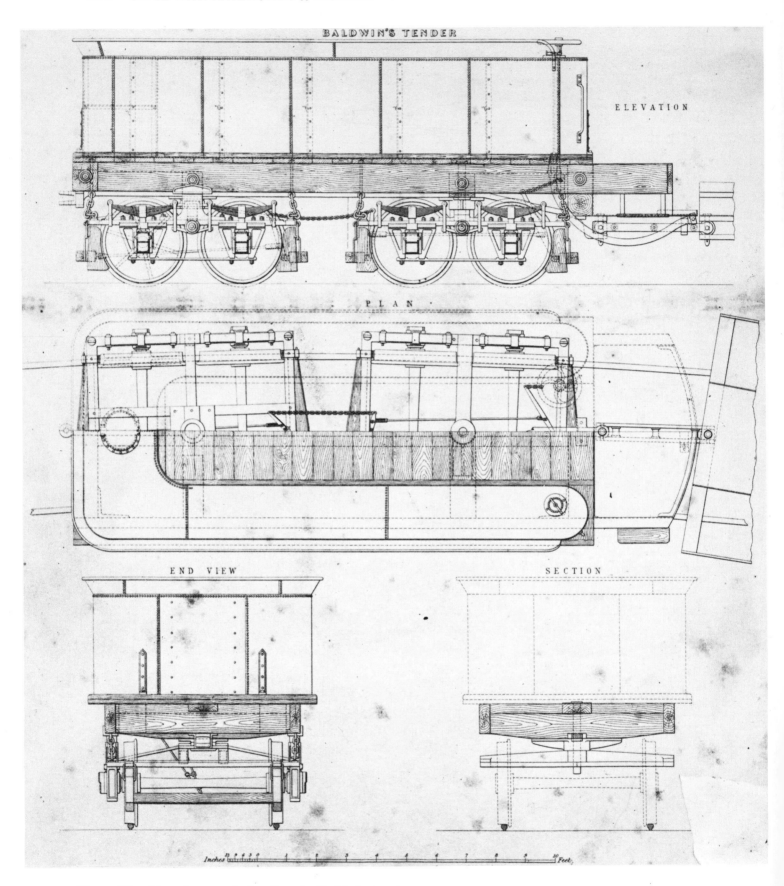

Figure 99. Elevations and plan for the Baldwin tender.

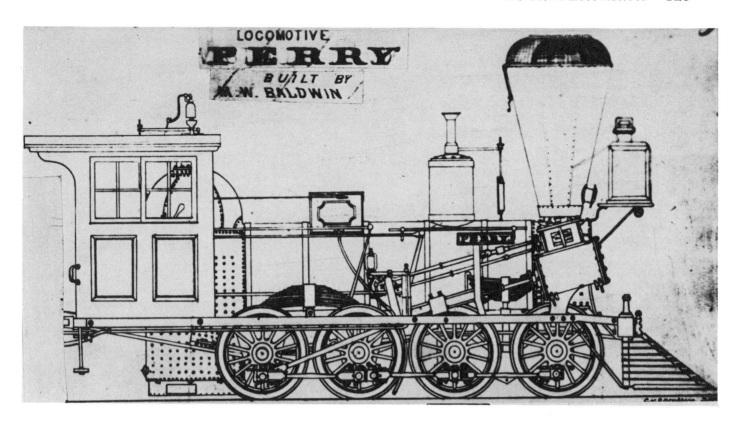

Figure 100.   The Pennsylvania Railroad's *Dauphin* and *Perry* were the first Baldwin engines on that road (1848). Both were the flexible-beam type. The drawing is ¼″ scale.

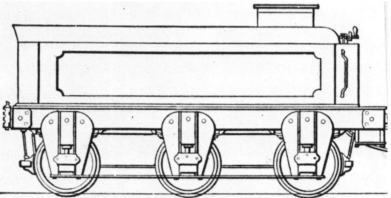

Figure 101. The *Armstrong* was another Baldwin-built Pennsylvania Railroad locomotive (1850). The drawing is ¼″ scale.

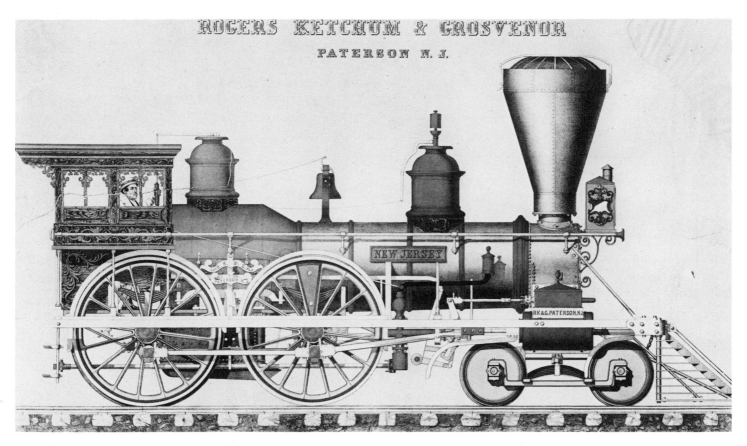

Figure 102. Rogers, Ketcham and Grosvenor built the *New Jersey* in 1852.

Figure 103. An old ¼″-scale drawing of the *Atalanta,* a Seth Wilmarth-built Pennsylvania engine of 1852.

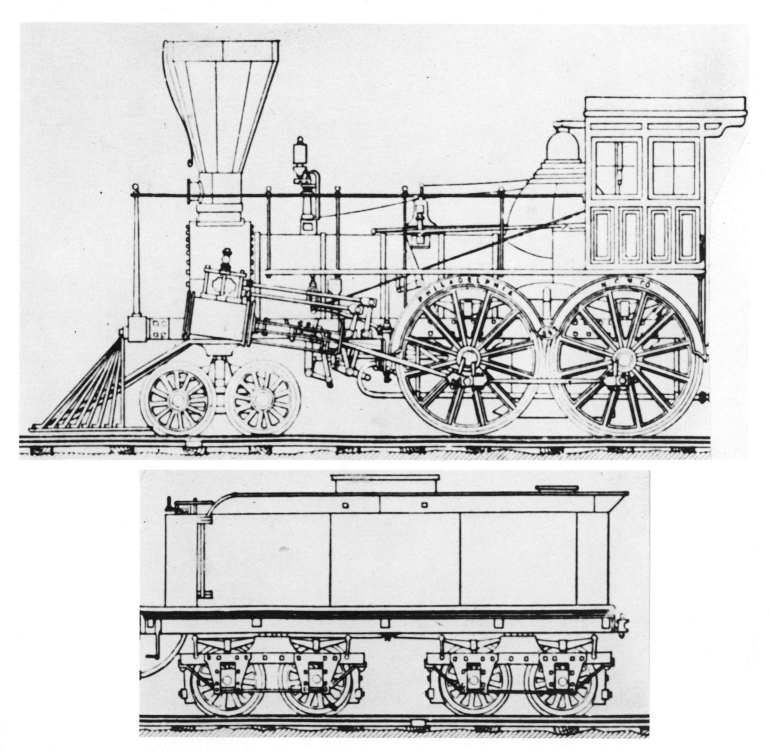

Figure 104. The *Philadelphia* of the Philadelphia, Wilmington & Baltimore Railroad was built by the Newcastle Manufacturing Co. of that city in Delaware in 1852.

Figure 105. A ¼"-scale reproduction of an advertising lithograph showing a Wm. Norris & Son's 4-4-0 of the 1850s.

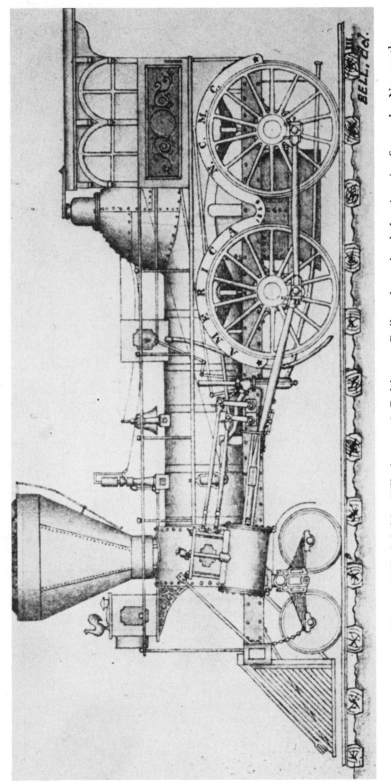

Figure 106. In 1854 the Philadelphia, Wilmington & Baltimore Railroad received the *America* from the Newcastle Manufacturing Co. The drawing is ¼" scale.

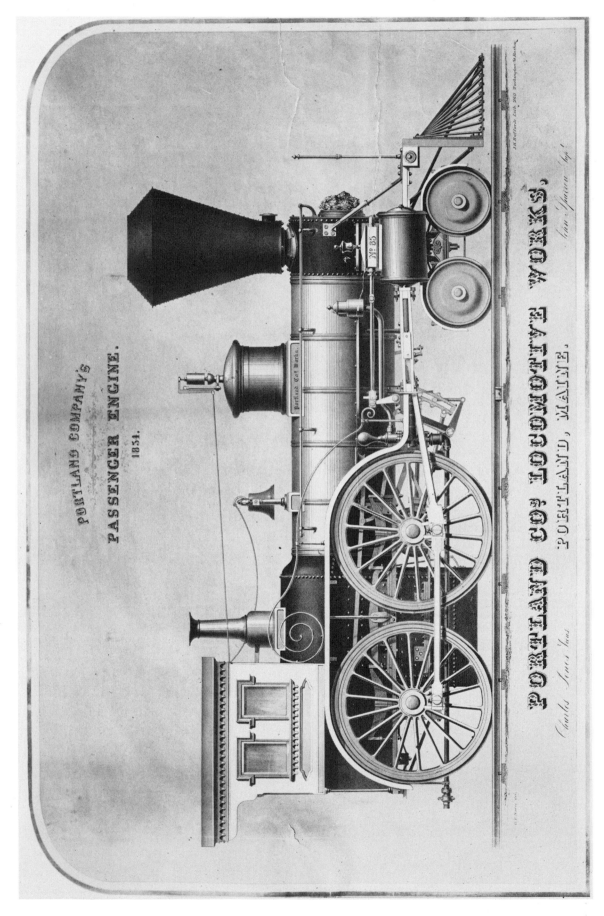

Figure 107. A ¼"-scale lithograph reproduction of No. 85 built by the Portland Company's Locomotive Works, Portland, Maine, 1854.

Figure 108. The *Saturn* built by the Amoskeag Manufacturing Co., Boston, in 1854. Larger than ¼″ scale.

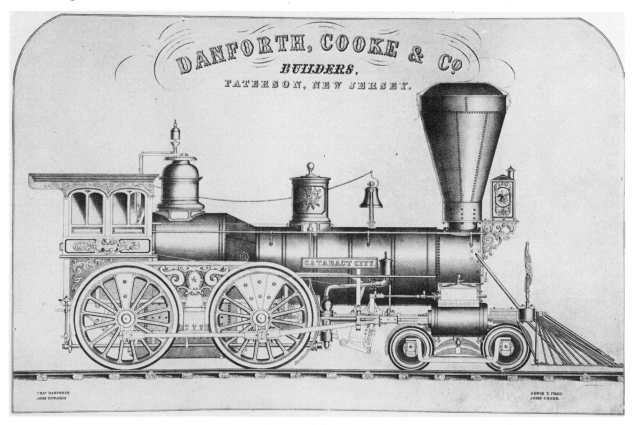

Figure 109. The *Cataract City* built by Danforth, Cooke & Co., Paterson, New Jersey, in 1855. Larger than ¼″ scale.

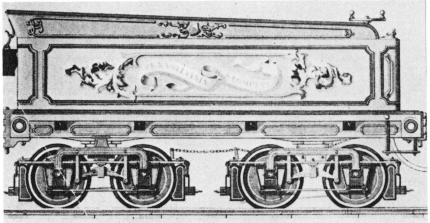

Figure 110. The *Tiger,* No. 134, of the Pennsylvania Railroad, built by Baldwin in 1856. The drawing is ¼″ scale.

Figure 111.   A model of the *Tiger*.

Figure 112.   The *Leopard,* sister engine of the *Tiger,* as it appeared with a few changes in 1869.

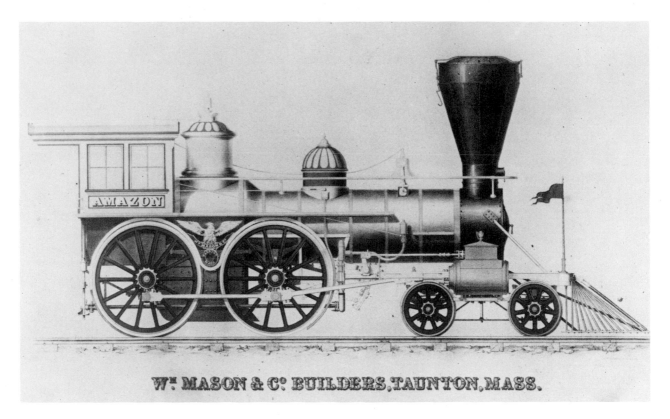

Figure 113. Wm. Mason & Co. built the *Amazon* in the 1850s. Larger than ¼″ scale.

Figure 114. A Baldwin lithograph of their *President* built for the Pennsylvania Railroad in 1859.

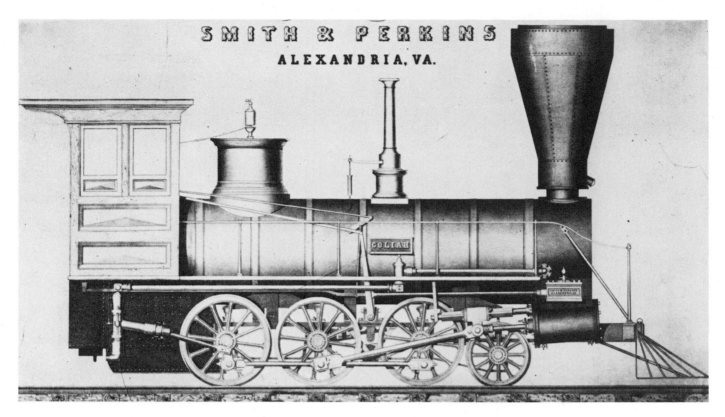

Figure 115. The *Goliah*, a Pennsylvania locomotive built by Smith & Perkins, 1856. The drawing is ¼″ scale.

Figure 116. The *Quigley*, No. 20, one of five similar engines built for the Louisville & Nashville in 1859 by Moore & Richardson, Cincinnati.

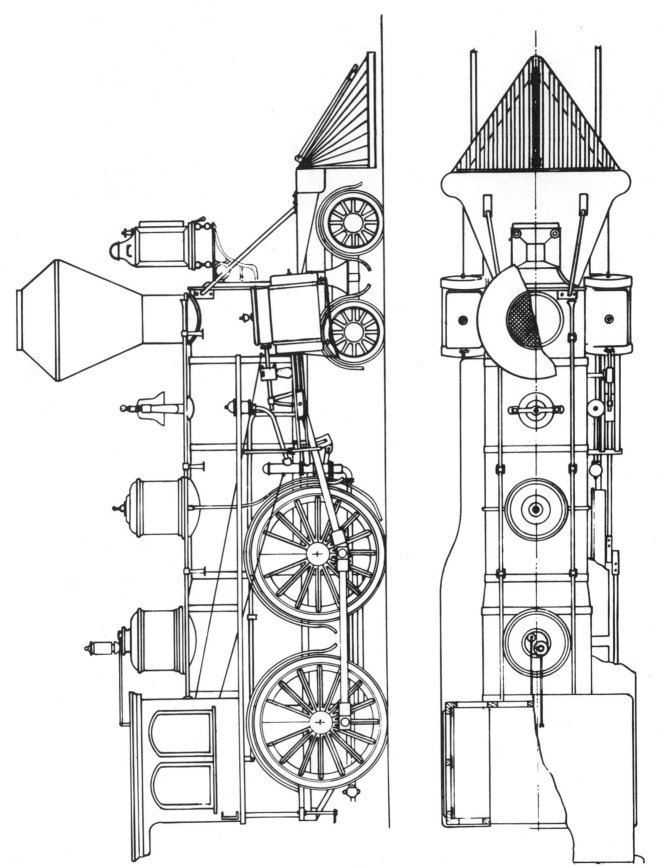

Figure 117. Right-side elevation and plan of the *Quigley,* ¼″ scale.

Figure 118. Views of the components of the model. *Top, left:* Smokebox front and stack. *Top, right:* Backhead, etc. *Below, left:* Cab and headlight. *Below, right:* Boiler, wheels, and other parts ready for assembly.

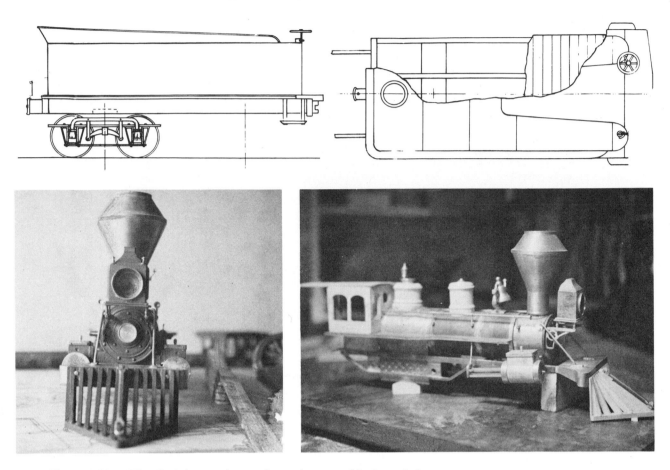

Figure 119. The *Quigley* tender and partly assembled model.

Figure 120. The finished model of the *Quigley* on exhibit at the Fort Donelson National Military Park near Dover, Tennessee.

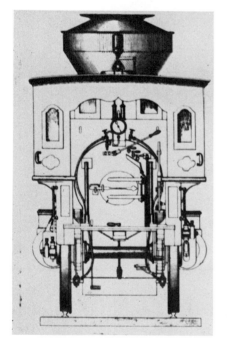

Figure 121. Top and bottom left: Side and end elevations, ¼" scale, of New Jersey Railroad and Transportation Co. engine No. 44. *Bottom, right:* Left-side photograph of same (1860s). Model by the author.

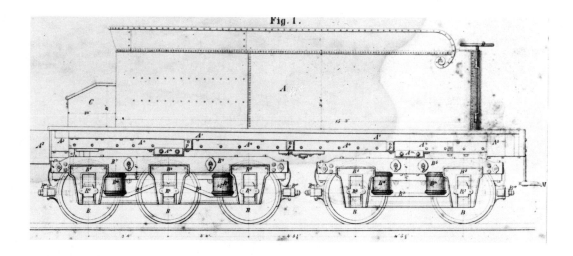

Fig. 1.

SIDE ELEVATION

Fig. 2.

TOP VIEW

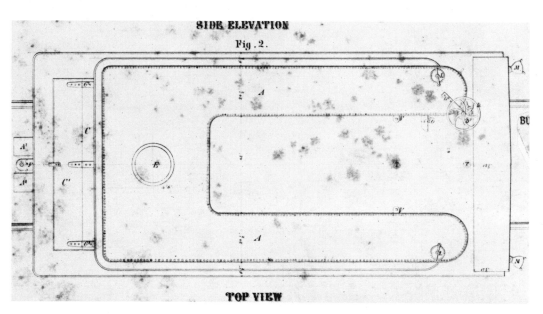

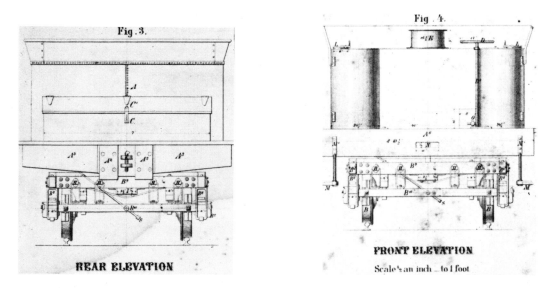

Fig. 3.

REAR ELEVATION

Fig. 4.

FRONT ELEVATION

Scale ¼ an inch _ to 1 foot

Figure 122.   Drawing of tender for No. 44, ¼″ scale.

Figure 123. The *Franklin,* a Cumberland Valley Railroad four-wheel switcher built by Baldwin, circa 1860.

Figure 124. A ¼″-scale model of an 1860s Pennsylvania engine.

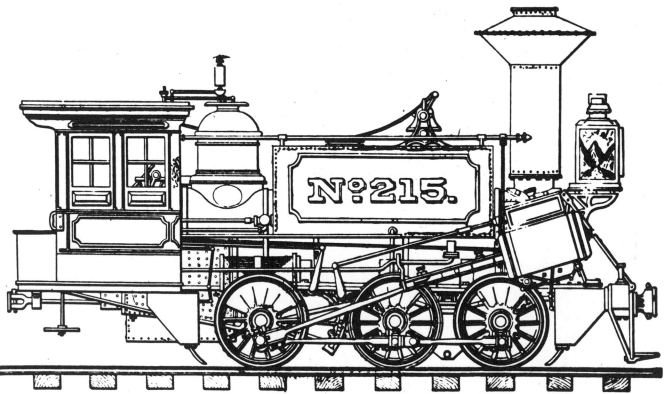

Figure 125.   Above: No. 216, a six-wheel Pennsylvania Railroad switcher built by Baldwin.
Below: A ¼″-scale side elevation.

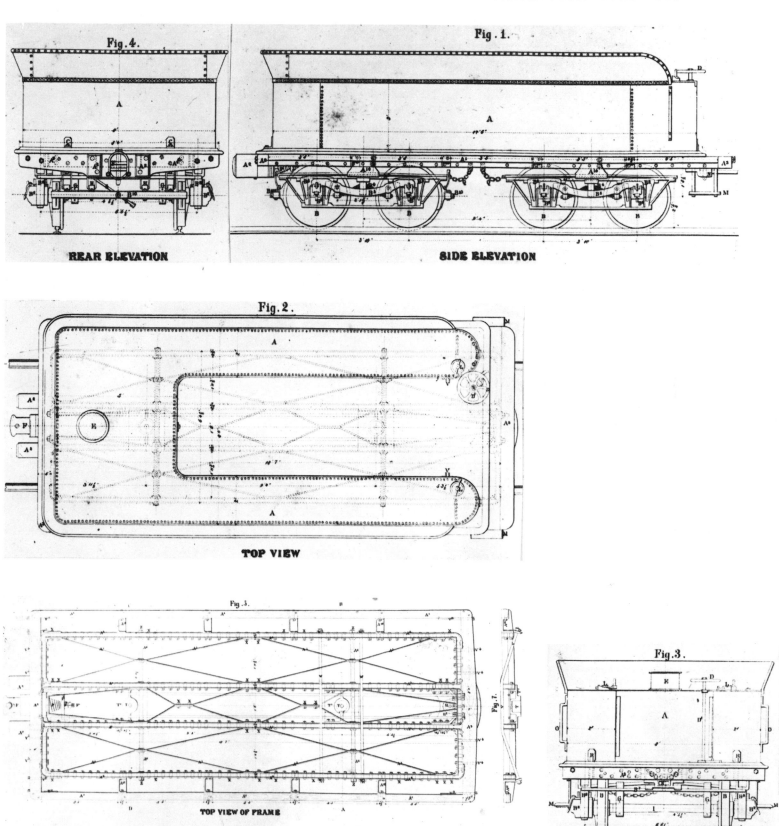

Figure 126. A representative tender of the 1860s by Danforth, Cooke; ¼″ scale.

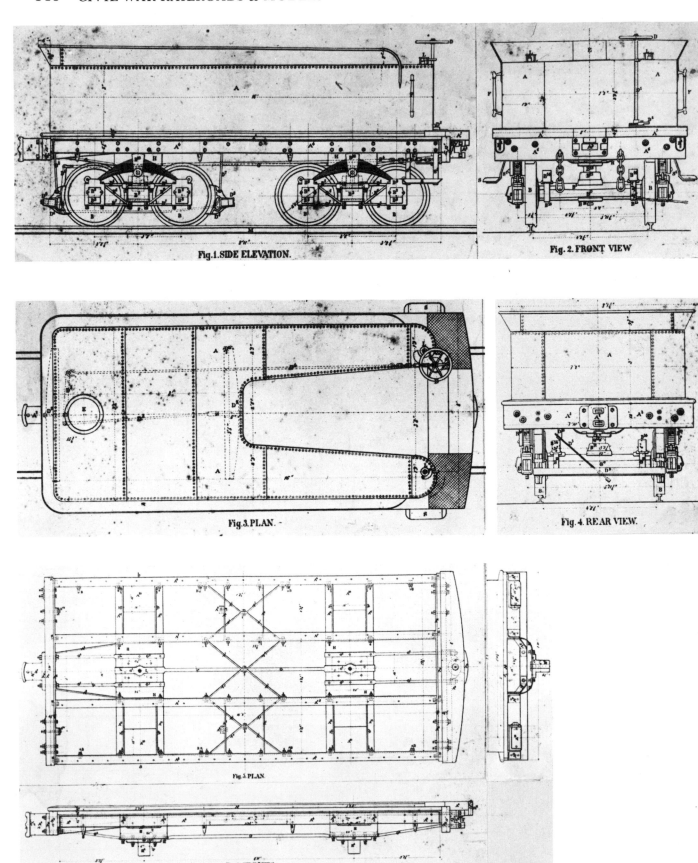

Fig.1. SIDE ELEVATION.

Fig. 2. FRONT VIEW

Fig. 3. PLAN.

Fig. 4. REAR VIEW.

Fig. 5. PLAN.

Fig. 6. SIDE VIEW
Scale ¼=1.

Figure 127. A tender by Hinkley; ¼″ scale.

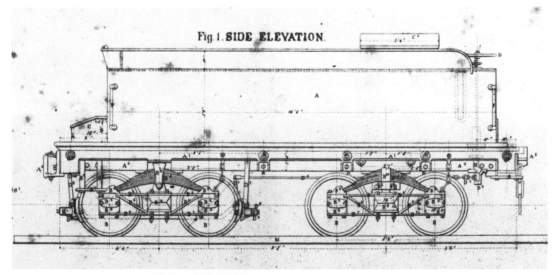

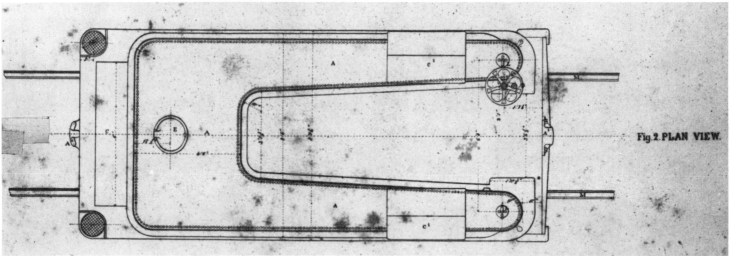

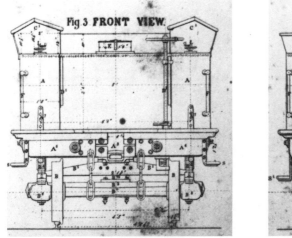

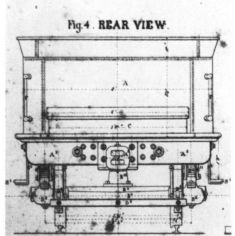

Figure 128. A Baldwin tender, ¼″ scale.

Figure 129. Pennsylvania Railroad No. 331, which pulled the Lincoln funeral train; as it appeared for that occasion.

Figure 130. No. 325, a sister engine of No. 331. One of twenty-one similar locomotives, built 1864.

CHAPTER VIII
Baltimore & Ohio Locomotives

T HE CHRONOLOGICAL RECORD OF EVENTS affecting the B & O during the first years of the war in Chapter I was obtained from the company's reports. Some of the following data pertaining to their motive power also came from this source and was amplified by Snowden Bell's writings (see Bibliography).

It is interesting that nearly all the B & O's early engines were still on their roster in 1860. Only four are not listed—the *Tom Thumb,* the *York,* the *Atlantic,* and the *Indian Chief* or *Traveler.* It is not likely that any of the "grasshopper" or "crab" types saw any service during the war, unless possibly yard work.

On April 18, 1861, General Stonewall Jackson took possession of Harper's Ferry, which he occupied until June 14, when he was ordered to destroy the bridges, the remains of the arsenal, and all facilities there, including the railroad. This was carried out, and a few days later he moved back to Martinsburg, demolishing on the way bridges, shops, and all railroad property.

It was then that Jackson conceived of appropriating some of the locomotives that the South so acutely needed. A forty-mile highway from Martinsburg to Strasburg was the only route to the rails of the Manassas Gap Railroad, and it was thus that Jackson planned the coup.

Thomas R. Sharp under Jackson's command was the organizer of personnel, horses, and equipment to move the engines over the road. On July twelfth the first, a 4-4-0, was jacked up and the lead trucks, rods, and heavier items were removed, as well as the driving wheels except the rear pair. The tender was moved separately. Wagons carried the dismantled parts. A wooden device with wide roller-type wheels replaced the lead or engine truck. With thirty-five men (in later moves as many as two hundred were mentioned) and forty horses four abreast the first engine was started on its way, reaching Strasburg in three days. The rest of the engines followed over a period of several months.

All the locomotives, except No. 34, whose boiler had been used in a Confederate gunboat, were recovered at the end of the war and returned to the Baltimore & Ohio.

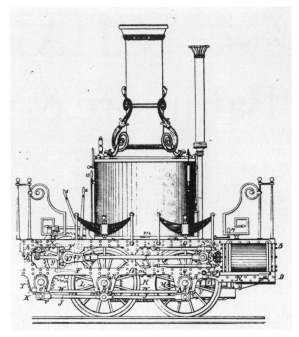

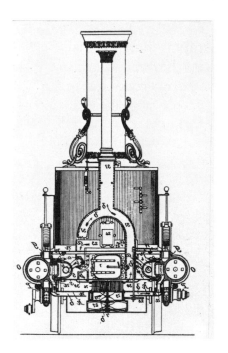

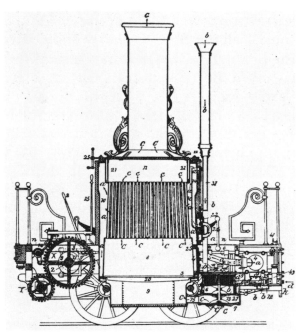

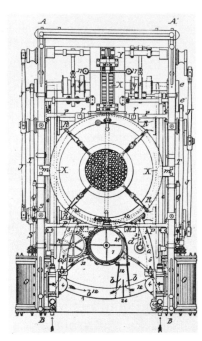

Figure 131. *Upper right:* No. 1, the *Arabian,* a "grasshopper" type by Winans. Other drawings of "crab"-type locomotive by Gillingham & Winans, ¼″ scale.

Locomotives Confiscated by General Jackson

Date	Number	Builder	Drivers	Type	
11/50	34 (2nd No. 34)	B & O	43"	0-8-0	8-wheel
12/47	50 ("Wisconisco")	Baldwin	43"	0-6-0	flexible beam truck
7/53	165	Denmead	50"	4-6-0	Hayes 10-wheeler
7/53	166	Denmead	50"	4-6-0	Hayes 10-wheeler
7/53	167	Denmead	50"	4-6-0	Hayes 10-wheeler
11/58	188	B & O	58"	4-4-0	"Lady Davis"
11/53	199	Denmead	50"	4-6-0	Hayes 10-wheeler
3/54	202	Denmead	50"	4-6-0	Hayes 10-wheeler
3/54	204	Denmead	50"	4-6-0	Hayes 10-wheeler
?/57	225	Denmead	50"	4-6-0	Tyson 10-wheeler
?/57	226	Denmead	50"	4-6-0	Tyson 10-wheeler
8/57	231	Mason	60"	4-4-0	Tyson 10-wheeler
8/57	235	Mason	60"	4-4-0	Tyson 10-wheeler

Baltimore & Ohio Railroad Company

(LOCOMOTIVES) MACHINERY DEPARTMENT REPORT, OCTOBER 1, 1860 (THATCHER PERKINS)

Date	Number	Name	Builder	Drivers	Type	
7/34	1	Arabian	Phineas Davis	35"	0-4-0	grasshopper
10/34	2	G. Washington	Gillingham & Winans	35"	0-4-0	grasshopper
6/35	3	T. Jefferson	Gillingham & Winans	35"	0-4-0	grasshopper
6/35	4	J. Madison	Gillingham & Winans	35"	0-4-0	grasshopper
7/35	5	J. Monroe	Gillingham & Winans	35"	0-4-0	grasshopper
2/36	6	J. Q. Adams	Gillingham & Winans	35"	0-4-0	grasshopper
4/36	7	A. Jackson	Gillingham & Winans	35"	0-4-0	grasshopper
8/36	8	J. Hancock	Gillingham & Winans	36"	0-4-0	crab
8/36	9	P. Davis	Gillingham & Winans	36"	0-4-0	crab
11/36	10	G. Clinton	Gillingham & Winans	36"	0-4-0	crab
4/37	11	M. Van Buren	Gillingham & Winans	36"	0-4-0	crab
4/37	12	B. Franklin	Gillingham & Winans	36"	0-4-0	crab
4/37	13	Lafayette	William Norris	48"	4-2-0	
6/37	14	W. Patterson	Gillingham & Winans	36"	0-4-0	crab
5/38	15	Isaac McKim	Gillingham & Winans	36"	0-4-0	crab
6/38	16	P. E. Thomas	W. M. Norris	48"	4-2-0	
10/38	17	Mazeppa	Gillingham & Winans	36"	0-4-0	crab
10/38	18	J. W. Patterson	Wm. Norris	48"	4-2-0	
12/38	19	Wm. Cooke	Wm. Norris	48"	4-2-0	
7/39	20	Patapsco	Wm. Norris	48"	4-2-0	
7/39	21	Monocacy	Wm. Norris	48"	4-2-0	
8/39	22	Potomac	Wm. Norris	48"	4-2-0	

Figure 132.   No. 37, the *Cumberland,* built by Winans, 1848.

Figure 133.   No. 51, the *Dragon,* a Baldwin-built engine of 1848.

Figure 134.   No. 54, the *Hero,* B & O-built, 1848.

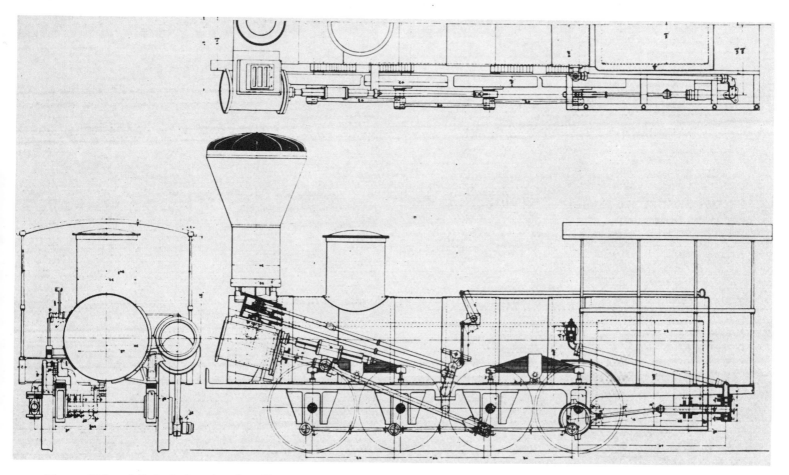

Figure 135.   A B & O drawing in ¼″ scale of a Baldwin 0-8-0 type 1848, such as the *Memnon* in Figure 136.

Figure 136.   No. 57, the *Memnon*, Baldwin-built, 1848.

B & O Locomotives in Service
Twenty Years Before the Civil War

Date	Number	Name	Builder	Drivers	Type	
9/39	23	Atlas	Eastwick & Harrison	60″	4-4-0	
11/39	24	Pegasus	Wm. Norris	60″	4-4-0	
12/39	25	Vesta	Wm. Norris	60″	4-4-0	
11/56	25 (2nd)		Wm. Mason	60″	4-4-0	
8/40	26	Vulcan	Eastwick & Harrison	60″	4-4-0	
11/56	26 (2nd)		Wm. Mason	60″	4-4-0	
2/40	27	Jupiter	Eastwick & Harrison	60″	4-4-0	
1/59	27 (2nd)		Taunton	60″	4-4-0	
7/41	28	Arrow	Newcastle	60″	4-4-0	
8/42	29	Mercury	Eastwick & Harrison	60″	4-4-0	
2/42	30	Minerva	Eastwick & Harrison	60″	4-4-0	
5/43	31	Stag	Wm. Norris	60″	4-4-0	
10/43	32	Atalanta	Winans	60″	4-4-0	
10/44	33	Hercules	Winans	33″	0-8-0	mud digger
10/50	33 (2nd)		B & O	43″	0-8-0	
11/44	34	Gladiator	Winans	33″	0-8-0	mud digger
11/50	34 (2nd)		B & O	43″	0-8-0	
11/34	35	Buffalo	Winans	33″	0-8-0	mud digger
12/50	35 (2nd)		B & O	43″	0-8-0	
12/44	36	Baltimore	Winans	33″	0-8-0	mud digger
8/45	37	Cumberland	Winans	33″	0-8-0	mud digger
8/45	38	Elephant	Winans	33″	0-8-0	mud digger
12/51	38 (2nd)		B & O	43″	0-8-0	
12/45	39	Reindeer	Winans	60″	4-4-0	
7/46	40	Opequan	Winans	33″	0-8-0	mud digger
4/51	40 (2nd)		B & O	43″	0-8-0	mud digger
7/46	41	Elk	Winans	43″	0-8-0	mud digger
10/46	42	Catoctin	Winans	43″	0-8-0	mud digger
10/60	42 (2nd)		B & O	60″	4-4-0	
11/46	43	Youghiogheny	Winans	33″	0-8-0	mud digger
4/52	43 (2nd)		B & O	43″	0-8-0	
12/46	44	Baldwin	Baldwin	43″	0-6-0	
12/46	45	Tuscarora	Winans	33″	0-8-0	mud digger
12/46	46	Allegheny	Winans	33″	0-8-0	mud digger
12/46	47	Newcastle	Newcastle	60″	4-4-0	
1/47	48	Delaware	Newcastle	60″	4-4-0	
5/47	49	Mount Clare	B & O	33″	0-8-0	mud digger
5/52	49 (2nd)		B & O	43″	0-8-0	
12/47	50	Wisconisco	Baldwin	43″	0-8-0	
1/48	51	Dragon	Baldwin	43″	0-8-0	
1/48	52	Juno	Winans	60″	4-4-0	
2/48	53	Unicorn	Baldwin	43″	0-6-0	
4/48	54	Hero	B & O	43″	0-8-0	
6/48	55	Camel	B & O	43″	0-8-0	camel (1st camel type)
6/48	56	Saturn	Newcastle	43″	0-8-0	
10/48	57	Memnon	Baldwin	43″	0-8-0	
12/48	58	Hector	Baldwin	43″	0-8-0	

Date	Number	Name	Builder	Drivers	Type	
12/48	59	Iris	Winans	43"	0-8-0	camel
12/48	60	Cossack	Baldwin	43"	0-8-0	
12/48	61	Mars	Winans	43"	0-8-0	camel
1/49	62	Tartar	Baldwin	43"	0-8-0	
5/49	63	Giant	B & O	43"	0-8-0	
3/50	64	Lion	B & O	43"	0-8-0	
9/50	65	Phoenix	Winans	43"	0-8-0	camel
9/50	66	Apollo	Winans	43"	0-8-0	camel
10/52	67	Tiger	B & O	43"	0-8-0	
10/50	68	Savage	Winans	43"	0-8-0	camel
10/50	69	Pilot	Winans	43"	0-8-0	camel
3/51	70		Winans	43"	0-8-0	camel
4/51	71		Winans	43"	0-8-0	camel
6/51	72		B & O	43"	0-8-0	camel
6/52	72 (2nd)		B & O	43"	0-8-0	
6/51	73–85		Winans	43"	0-8-0	camel
3/51	76		B & O	43"	0-8-0	
8/51	77–82		Winans	43"	0-8-0	camel
10/51	83		B & O	43"	0-8-0	
9/53	83 (2nd)		Winans	43"	0-8-0	camel
1/52	84–88		Winans	43"	0-8-0	camel
1/52	89		B & O	60"	4-4-0	Dutch wagon, inside connected
3/52	90–94		Winans	43"	0-8-0	camel
3/52	95		B & O	60"	4-4-0	Dutch wagon, inside connected
5/52	96–98		Winans	43"	0-8-0	camel
6/52	99		B & O	60"	4-4-0	Dutch wagon, inside connected
8/52	100–106		Winans	43"	0-8-0	camel
9/52	107		B & O	60"	4-4-0	Dutch wagon, inside connected
10/52	108–121		Winans	43"	0-8-0	camel
?/63	117 (2nd)		B & O	64½"	4-6-0	first of Perkins 10-wheelers
12/52	122		Newcastle	60"	4-4-0	
1/53	123–125		Winans	43"	0-8-0	camel
1/53	126		R. Norris & Sons	60"	4-4-0	
1/53	127		R. Norris & Sons	60"	4-4-0	
6/53	128		Winans	43"	0-8-0	camel
7/53	129		B & O	52"	4-6-0	Hayes 10-wheeler
2/53	130		Winans	43"	0-8-0	camel
2/53	131		B & O	43"	0-8-0	
11/53	132–137		Winans	43"	0-8-0	camel
?/63	136 (2nd)		B & O	58"	4-6-0	Perkins 10-wheeler
5/53	138		Denmead	50"	4-6-0	Hayes 10-wheeler
5/53	139		Newcastle	50"	4-6-0	Hayes 10-wheeler

4/53	140	Winans	43″	0-8-0	camel
5/53	141	Winans	43″	0-8-0	camel
5/53	142	Smith & Perkins	50″	4-6-0	Hayes 10-wheeler
7/53	143–148	Winans	43″	0-8-0	camel
?/63	147	B & O	50″	4-6-0	Perkins 10-wheeler
7/53	149–153	Lawrence	60″	4-4-0	
7/53	154–157	Winans	43″	0-8-0	camel
7/53	158	Smith & Perkins	50″	4-6-0	Hayes 10-wheeler
7/53	159	Denmead	50″	4-6-0	Hayes 10-wheeler
7/53	160–163	Winans	43″	0-8-0	camel
7/53	164	Newcastle	60″	4-4-0	
7/53	165–167	Denmead	50″	4-6-0	
11/53	168–187	Winans	43″	0-8-0	camel
11/58	188	B & O	60″	4-4-0	
11/58	189–197	Winans	43″	0-8-0	camel
12/54	198	B & O	50″	4-6-0	Hayes 10-wheeler
11/53	199	Denmead	52″	4-6-0	
?/63	199 (2nd)	B & O	43″	0-8-0	camel
11/53	200	R. Norris	60″	4-4-0	Dutch wagon inside connected
1/54	201	R. Norris	60″	4-4-0	Dutch wagon, inside connected
1/54	202	Denmead	50″	4-6-0	Hayes 10-wheeler
1/54	203	B & O	50″	4-6-0	Hayes 10-wheeler
3/54	204	Denmead	50″	4-6-0	Hayes 10-wheeler
4/54	205	Denmead	50″	4-6-0	Hayes 10-wheeler
6/54	206	B & O	50″	4-6-0	Hayes 10-wheeler
11/54	207	Murray & Hazlehurst	60″	4-4-0	Dutch wagon inside connected
11/54	208	Murray & Hazlehurst	60″	4-4-0	Dutch wagon, inside connected
11/54	209	Denmead	60″	4-6-0	Hayes 10-wheeler
2/57	210–219	Winans	43″	0-8-0	camel
2/57	220	Denmead	60″	4-4-0	
2/57	221	Denmead	60″	4-4-0	
4-12/57	222-228	Denmead	50″	4-6-0	Tyson 10-wheeler
10/57	229	B & O	50″	4-6-0	Tyson 10-wheeler
10/57	230	B & O	50″	4-6-0	Tyson 10-wheeler
8/57	231–236	Mason	60″	4-4-0	Tyson 10-wheeler
65-66	237–241	B & O	66″	4-4-0	Perkins passenger engines
?/63	9, 13, 14, 18, 19, 29, 35, 36, 136, 147 (new numbers)	B & O			Perkins 10-wheelers

Figure 137. A three-quarter front view of the *Memnon*. This old drawing has been incorrectly titled *Dragon* on the cab.

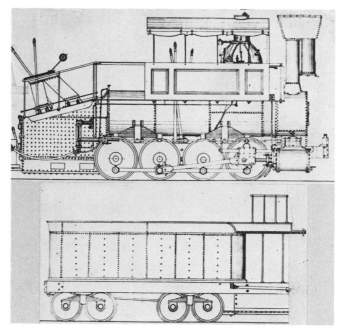

Figure 138. A ⅛″-scale side elevation of a Winans *Camel* locomotive of 1853, with its tender. J. Snowden Bell drawing, 1896.

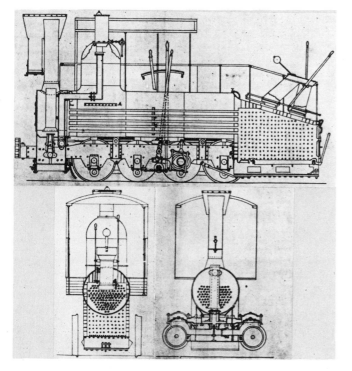

Figure 139. *Camel* engine sections, ⅛″ scale.

Figure 140. No. 80, an 1851 *Camel*, photographed years later.

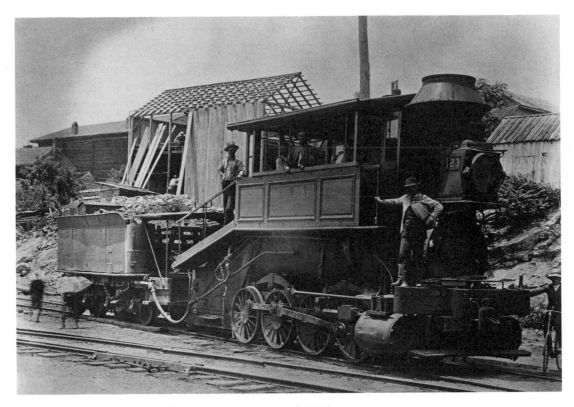

Figure 141. No. 123, a Winans *Camel* of 1853.

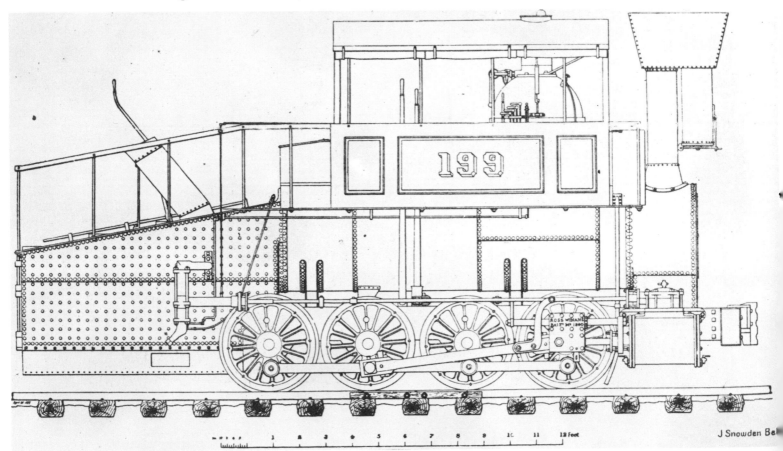

Figure 142. No. 199, last of the *Camel* engines. Note the extended firebox. ¼″-scale drawing.

Figure 143. A ¼″-scale imported model of a *Camel* engine. Note that the firebox is not according to the prototype, nor are some other details.

Figure 144. No. 139, a Hayes ten-wheel *Camel* built by Newcastle in 1853.

Figure 145.   No. 198, a Hayes ten-wheel *Camel* built by the B & O in 1854.

Figure 146.   No. 201, a "Dutch wagon" type built by R. Norris & Son, 1854.

Figure 147.   No. 207, a "Dutch wagon" built by Murray & Hazlehurst, 1854.

Figure 148. No. 25 (the second 25) built by Wm. Mason, 1856.

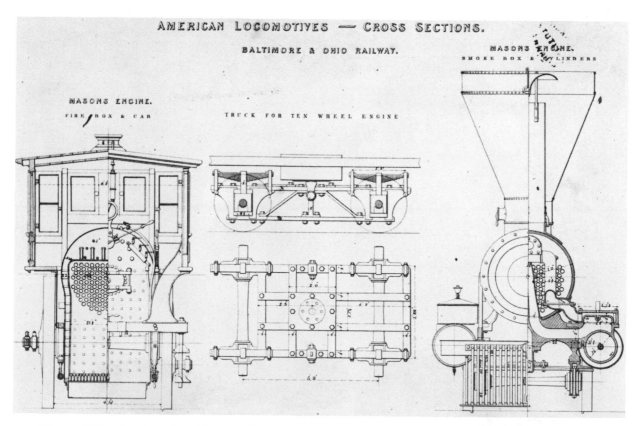

Figure 149. Sections in ¼″ scale of Mason locomotives, and a truck for a ten-wheel locomotive.

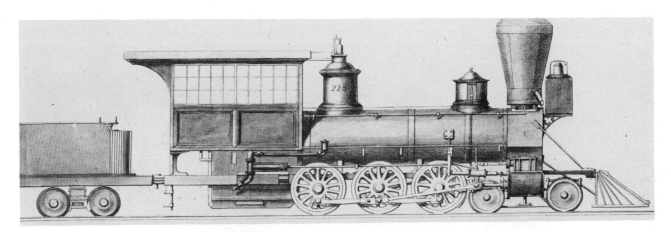

Figure 150. A version of the Tyson ten-wheeler.

Figure 151. No. 188, a Tyson 4-4-0 built by the B & O. Smaller than ¼″ scale.

Figure 152. No. 117, drawing of a Perkins ten-wheeler. Smaller than ¼″-scale.

Figure 153. No. 261, an eight-wheel engine, 1863.

Figure 154. No. 32 (originally No. 83), an eight-wheel locomotive B & O built in 1865.

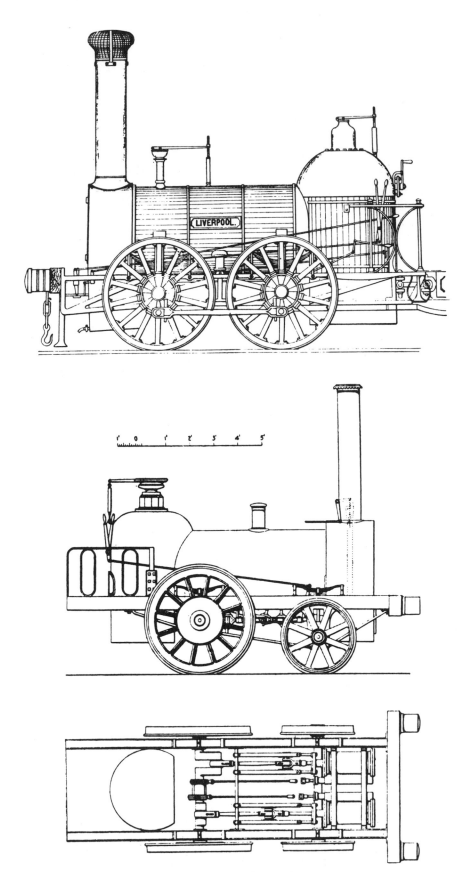

Figure 155. Above: The *Liverpool,* built by Edward Bury. *Below:* The *Pioneer,* built by Rothwell, Hicks and Rothwell in England for the Petersburg Railroad. Both had 54″-diameter driving wheels. The *Liverpool* arrived in 1833, the *Pioneer* in 1832. Drawings ¼″ scale.

CHAPTER IX
Southern Locomotives

THE LOCOMOTIVES of the South were few in number compared with those of the North. Most, such as the famous *General*, as well as the *Texas* and *Yonah*, involved in the "Great Locomotive Chase," had been built by Northern manufacturers. Among the drawings and photographs in this section are two engines built by the Tredegar Iron Works of Richmond: the *Roanoke* for the Virginia and Tennessee Railroad in 1854 and the *Alleghany* for the Virginia Central Railroad in 1856 (Figures 159 and 173).

Line drawings of Southern locomotives imported from England that precede those built in Civil War times are also included. One at least, the *Raleigh*, is known to have been in service as late as 1857 (Figure 157).

Drawings in ¼″ scale of the General as it appeared when built and at the time of the Andrews Raid are seen in Figures 166 and 167. These agree with the research and painting of Wilbur Kurtz (Figure 164), the outstanding authority on these engines. When compared with Figure 165, the *General*, as it was rebuilt at various times, is hardly recognizable as the same engine. The horizontal bar outside the driving wheels is not an outside frame, as it is sometimes mistakenly called, but the angle rail (colloquially, "ankle rail"), the forerunner of the runningboard.

Figure 156. A full-scale replica of the *Raleigh*. Originally on the Petersburg Railroad, later on the Raleigh & Gaston Railroad. It was still running in 1857. The parent road is now part of the Seaboard Coast Line.

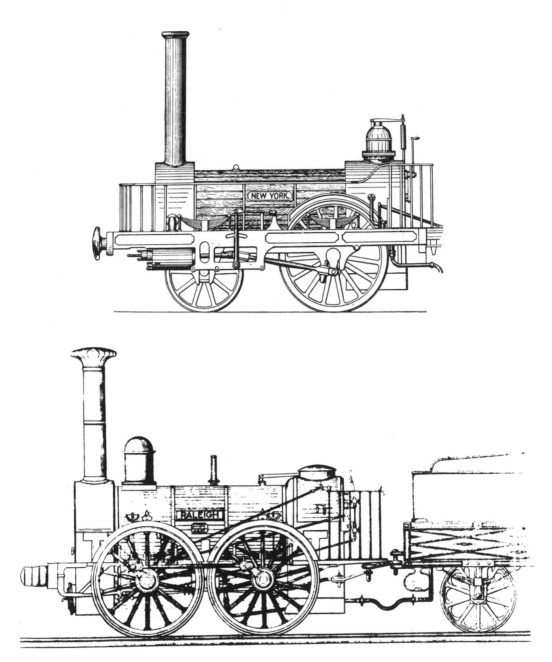

Figure 157. *Above:* The *New York*, built by Mather Dixon & Co., 1833; ¼″ scale. *Below:* The *Raleigh*, No. 10, built by Tayleur & Co., 1836, ¼″ scale.

Figure 158. The *Westward Ho* was built by the Norris Bros. for the Virginia Central Railroad in 1848. It is now part of the Chesapeake & Ohio. The photograph was made in 1870.

Figure 159. The *Roanoke* of the Virginia & Tennessee Railroad was built by the Tredegard Iron Works at Richmond in 1854.

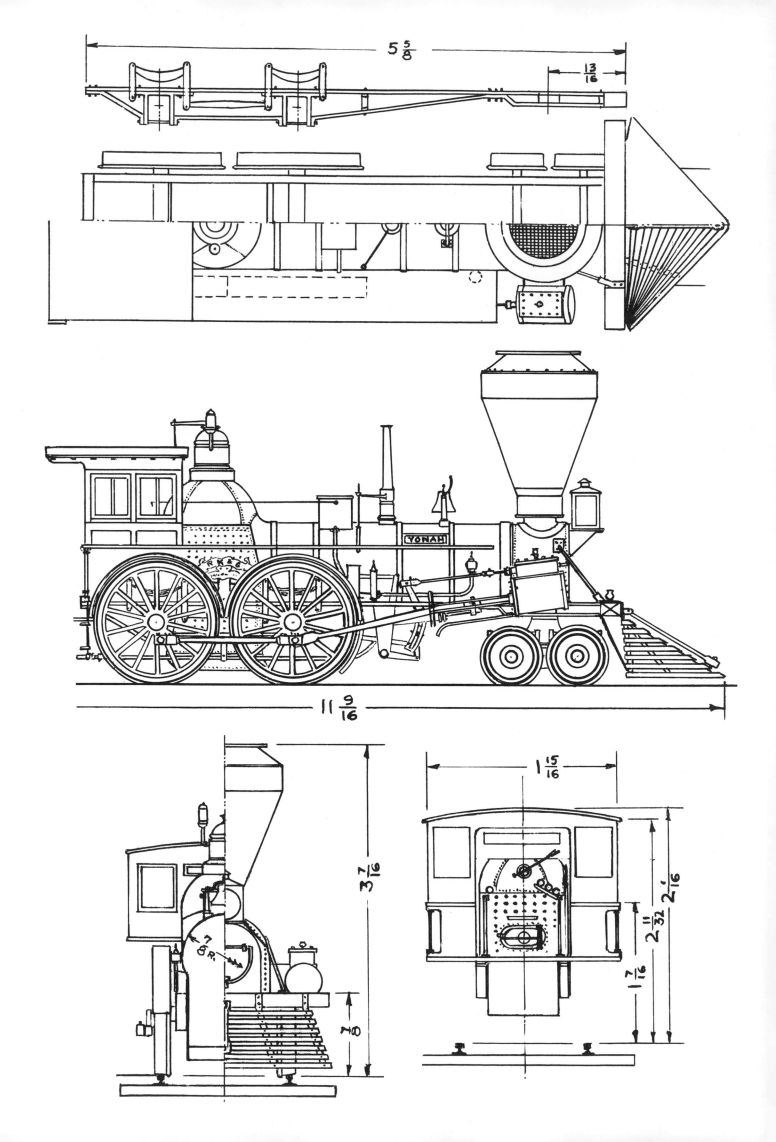

YONAH

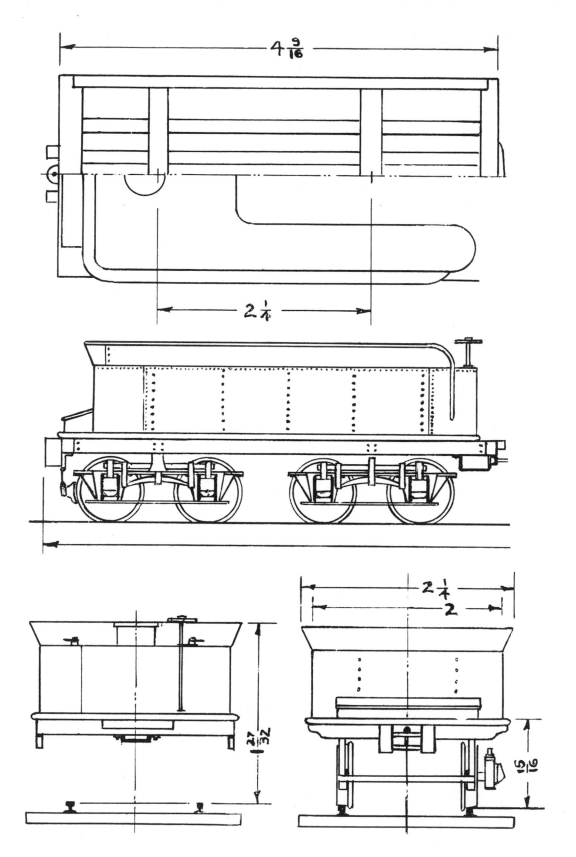

Figure 161. Tender for the *Yonah,* based on Rogers data; ¼″ scale.

Figure 160. *Opposite:* The *Yonah,* elevations and plan in ¼″ scale. Drawing by the author.

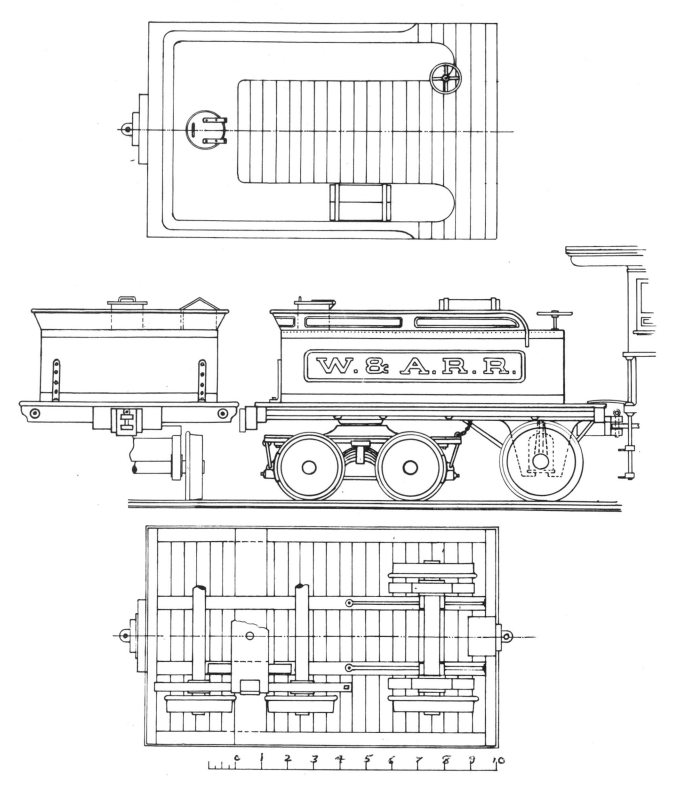

Figure 162. Tender for the *Yonah* as sketched by Wilbur Kurtz, completed by the author. This six-wheel tender may have replaced the eight-wheel one, but this has not been verified.

Figure 163. The *John T. Souter,* a Rogers engine very similar to the *General* built for the Nashville & Chattanooga Railroad about the same year as the *General.* The *General*'s iron driving wheels were 60″ in diameter, the *Souter*'s 54″. The tender trucks were identical.

Figure 164. The *General,* from a Wilbur Kurtz painting. Compare this with the next illustration. This famous locomotive was built by Rogers in 1855.

Figure 165. The *General* as rebuilt and as it appeared from the 1880s on.

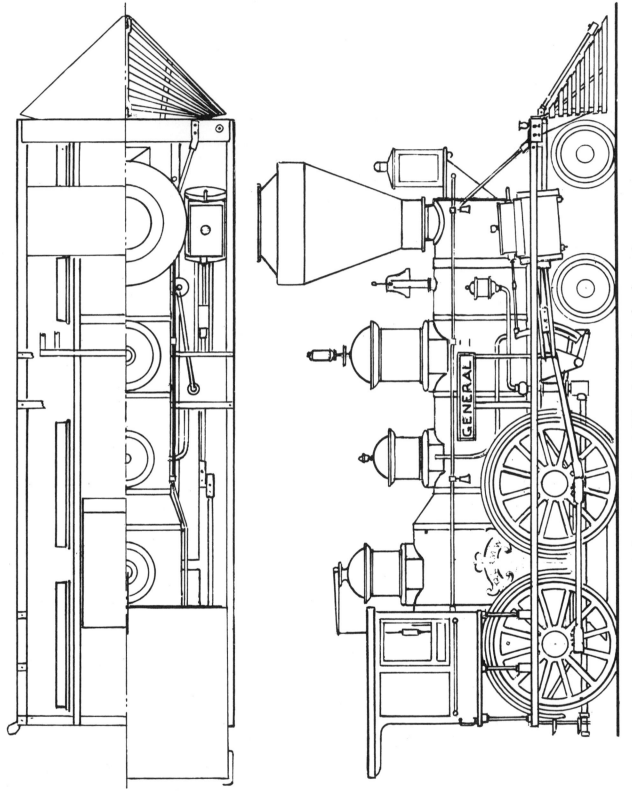

Figure 166. The elevation and plan of the *General*; ¼" scale. Drawing by the author.

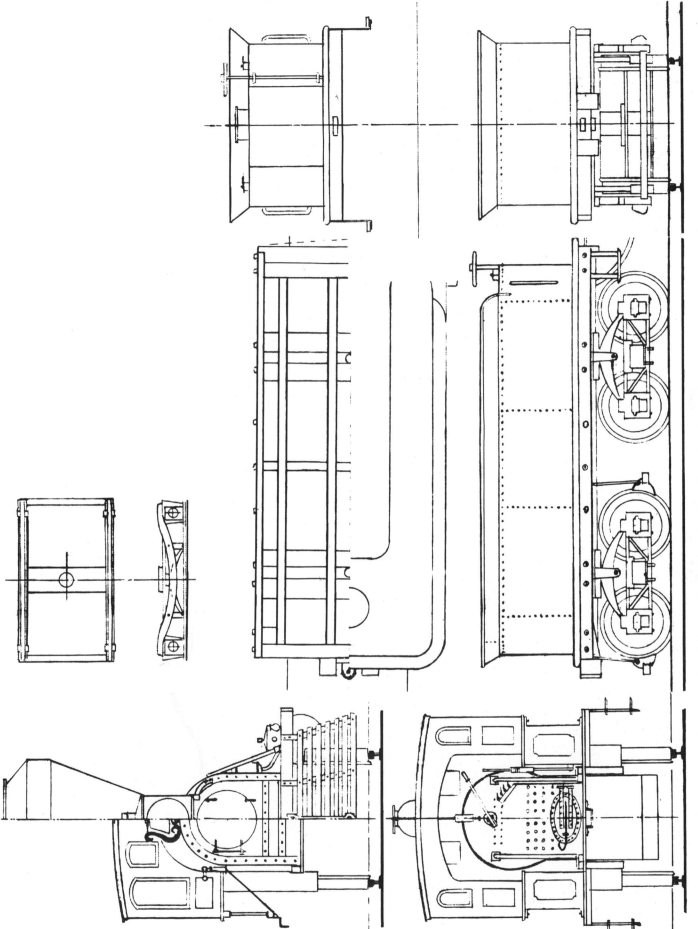

Figure 167. Elevations of the *General* and its tender; ¼" scale. Drawings by the author.

Figure 168. The *Texas* as researched and painted by Wilbur Kurtz.

Figure 169. The *Texas* as it appears today.

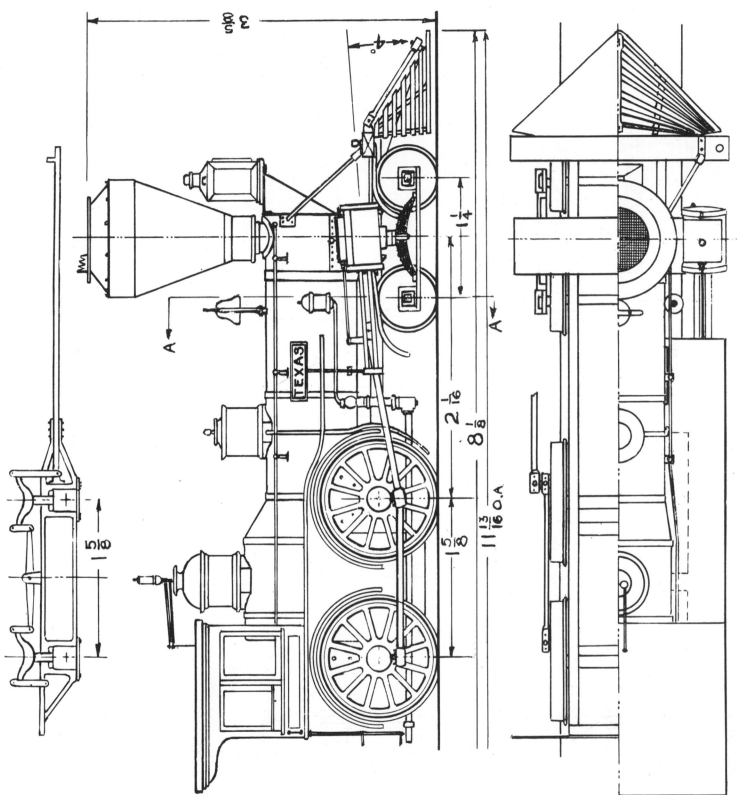

Figure 170. The *Texas*, elevation and plan in ¼" scale. Drawing by the author.

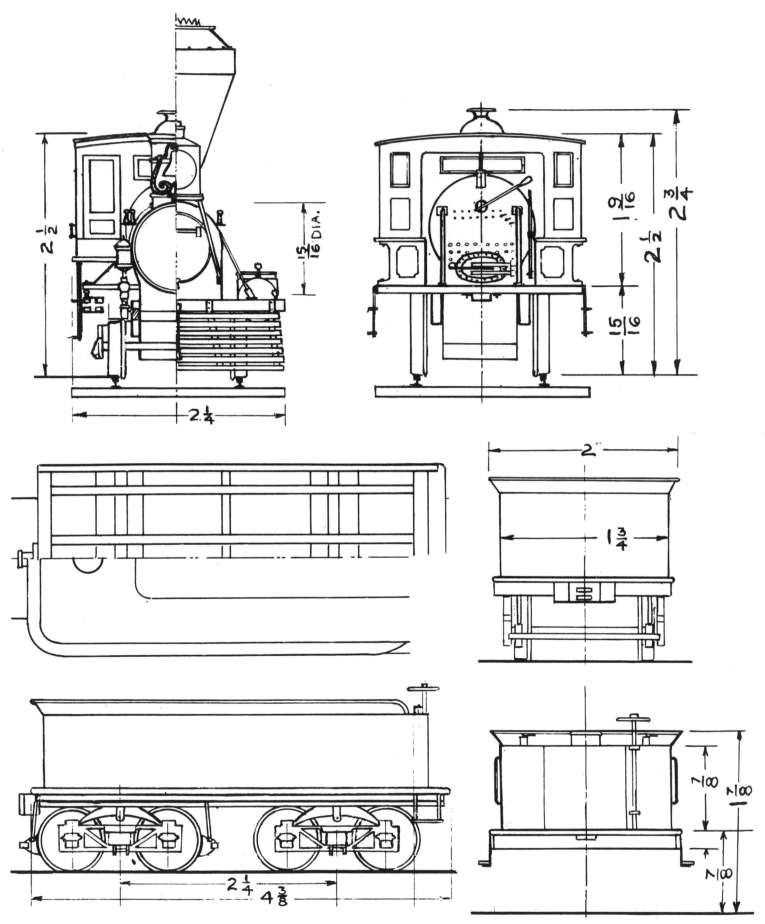

Figure 171. The *Texas*, sections and elevation and plan of its tender; ¼″ scale.

Figure 172. The *Virginia,* from an old lithograph; a shade under ¼″ scale. It was built in 1856 by the Virginia Locomotive and Car Manufacturing Co. of Alexandria and was possibly the only engine they built.

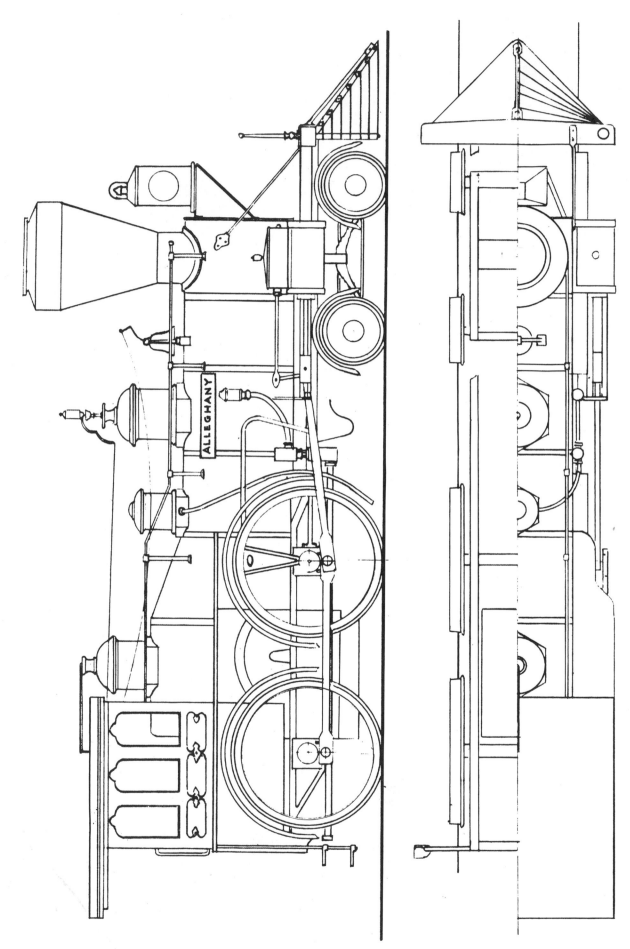

Figure 173. The *Alleghany* was built by the Tredegar Iron Works for the Virginia Central Railroad in 1856. ¼" scale. Drawing by the author.

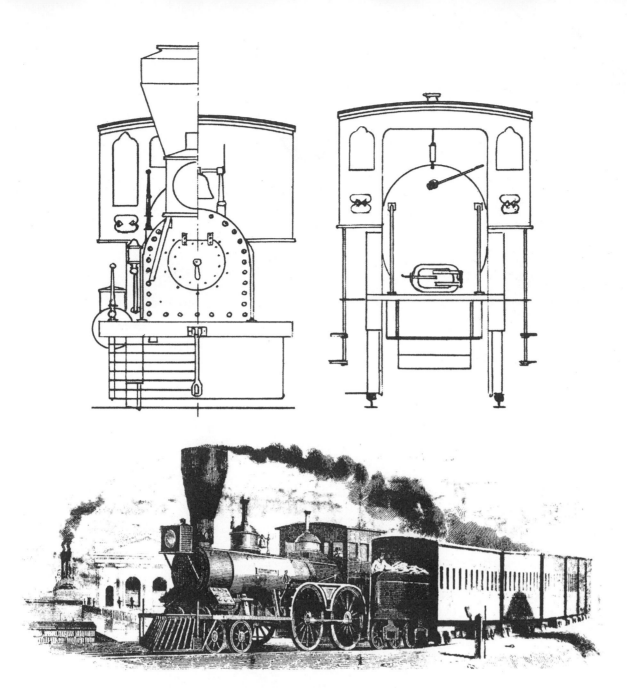

Figure 174. *Top:* Alleghany sections. *Middle:* A Greenville and Columbia Railroad train of the late 1850s. *Bottom:* An unidentified train also in the 1850s.

Figure 175. The *W. C. Gatewood,* a ten-wheeler built by Baldwin in 1859 for the South Carolina Railroad. This road had sixty-two locomotives in 1861.

Figure 176. The *Andy Johnson,* of the Virginia Central Railroad, built by Wm. Mason.

Figure 177. *Above:* The *Quincy,* similar to the *Souter* built by Rogers. *Below:* The *Lafourche* of the New Orleans & Gulf Railroad.

CHAPTER X
Passenger Cars

BEGINNING WITH AN 1845 PASSENGER COACH, a number of drawings of several types of other coaches follow. Cars of ten or more years before the Civil War were of course still in use. None were then what could be called standard, though the larger railroads such as the Baltimore & Ohio and the Pennsylvania were reaching that point. All were built of wood, even to the truck frames. Models of these cars should be similarly constructed, though it is not necessary to carry the idea as far as the trucks, a variety of which are obtainable.

As with miniature building construction, the actual cutting out of windows in coach sides is not necessary; the assembly of accurately cut wooden pieces is far simpler. Actually, a side of a car consists of a two-layer assembly. The underpiece, which becomes the inner wall, has window openings that will represent the sash. Thus, when the outer layer is applied—window posts, letterboard, belt rail, and lower side—it forms the rest of the side, including whatever trim is desired. Below the belt rail (the longitudinal strip under the windows) the side can represent board and batten or siding that comes in various widths in basswood. Most of the car models illustrated have siding, though the hospital car has the board and batten type.

The car ends can be made like the sides, with the door thickness being the lower or bottom piece. All four pieces—sides and ends—can then be assembled as a unit. Many car models used to be made with removable roofs, but assembling them on the body makes a better job, allowing easier interior detailing on the floor and the addition of lights in the ceiling if desired.

The floor should be a snug fit into the car unit so that its bottom will be flush with the bottom edges of the sides. A narrow portion the size of the platform should project at both

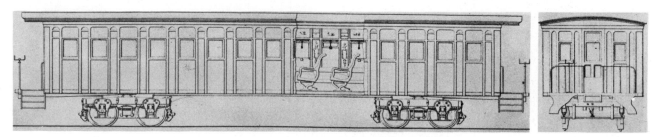

Figure 178a.   A B & O coach of 1856.

181

ends. There are various step and platform components available as well as link-and-pin couplers to keep everything to scale and in the right period. These couplers operate well in use, though the coupling and uncoupling require a bit of patience.

Passenger Rolling Stock as of 1860

BALTIMORE & OHIO RAILROAD

Smokers, Baggage, Express, Mail, etc.,	30
Passenger	51
Pay	1
Officers'	3
Street	1
Sleeping	4
Baggage	1
Total:	91

PENNSYLVANIA RAILROAD

8 wheel wide passenger	64
8 wheel narrow passenger	23
8 wheel emigrant	37
8 wheel baggage	35
8 wheel express	8
Total:	167

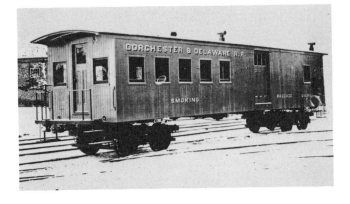

Figure 178b.   A coach a few years later in front of its builders, Jackson & Sharp, Wilmington, Delaware.

Figure 179.   *Above, right:* A Dorchester & Delaware combine coach of the 1860s. *Below, right:* An old coach of the Housatonic Railroad.

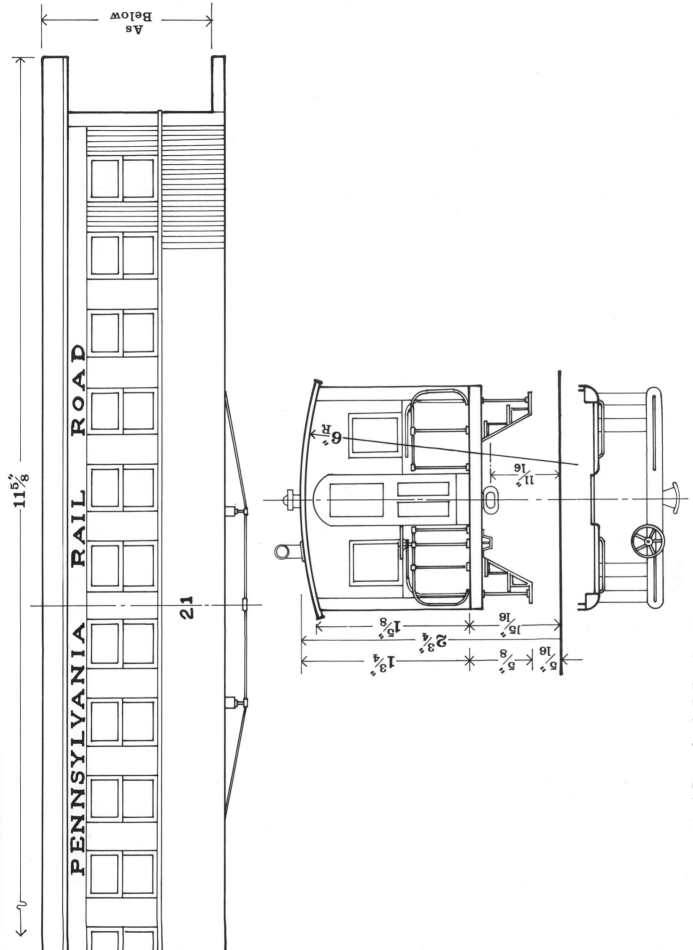

Figure 180. A Pennsylvania Railroad coach from the 1860s; ¼″ scale.

Figure 18l. Two ¼″-scale Pennsylvania 1860s models, a coach and a baggage car, by the author.

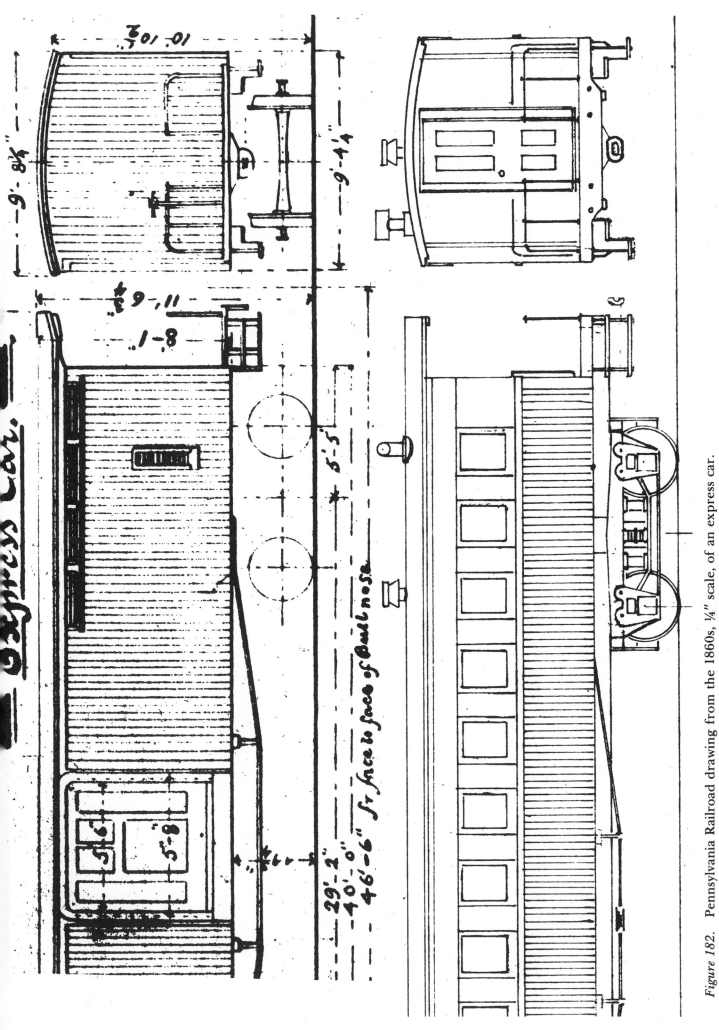

Express Car.

10' 10½"

9' 8½"

9' 4¼"

11' 9⅜"

8' 1"

5' 5"

3' 6"   5' 8"

29' 2"

40' 0"

46' 6" Fr face to face of Bull nose

Figure 182. Pennsylvania Railroad drawing from the 1860s, ¼" scale, of an express car.

Figure 183. *Below:* Elevation and end of a P. R. R. coach from which the models illustrated were made; ¼" scale.

Figure 184. An early photograph of a Pennsylvania passenger car end.

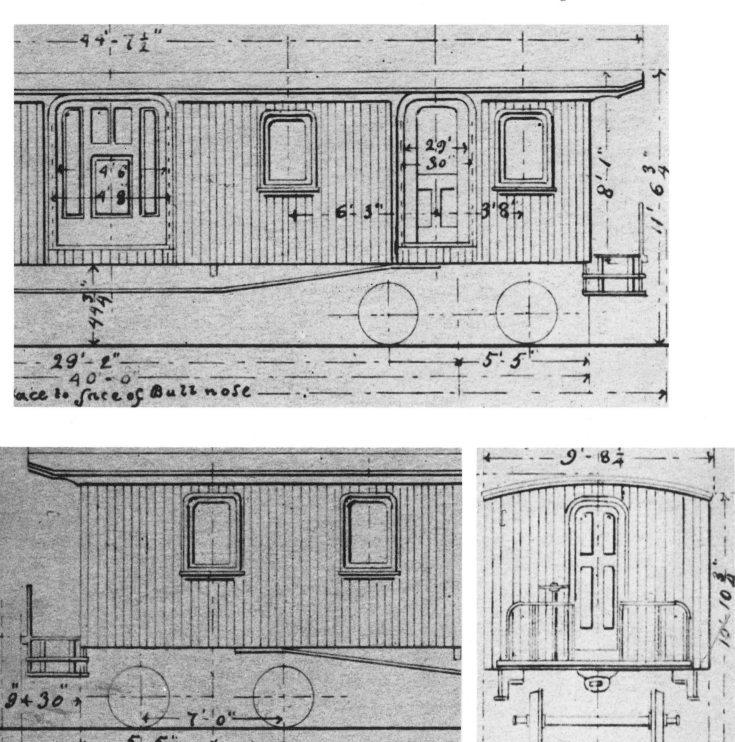

Figure 185. A ¼″-scale drawing of an 1860s P. R. R. baggage and mail car.

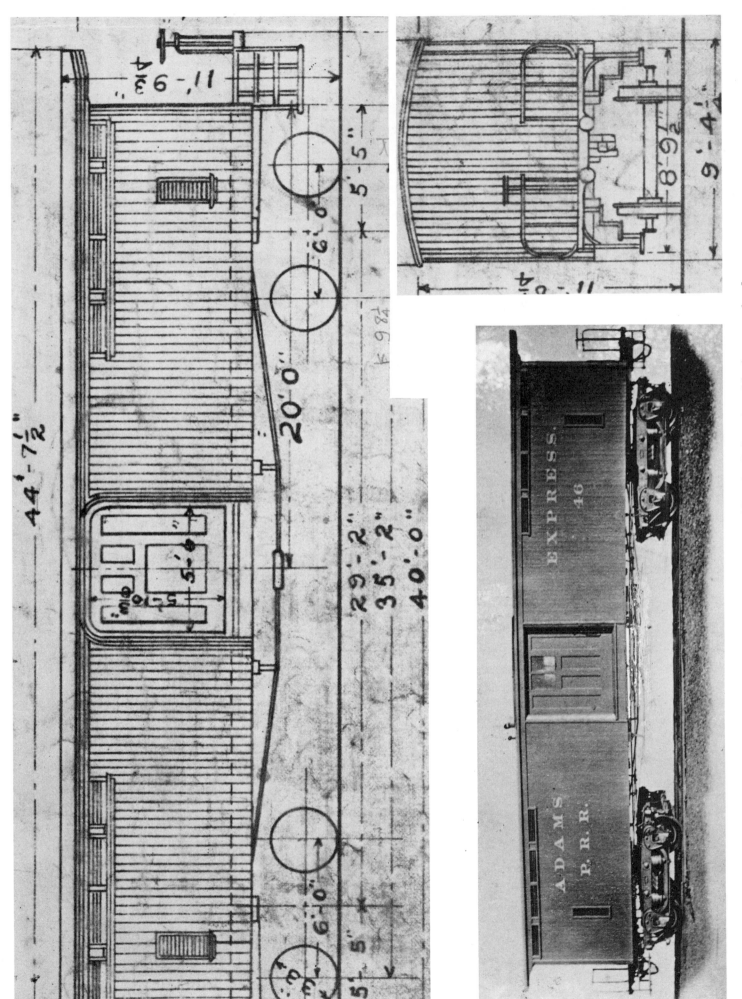

Figure 186. Above: A Pennsylvania drawing of a baggage or express car; ¼" scale. *Below:* An old photograph of an Adams Express car.

Figure 187. *Above:* A ¼″-scale model of an Orange & Alexandria Railroad coach. *Below:* Components of ¼″-scale passenger car model.

Figure 188. Two B & O cars of the 1860s. *Above:* Coach No. 20. *Below:* Baggage car No. 10.

Figure 189. Model of one of the first hospital cars; ¼″ scale.

Figure 190. A ¼″-scale model of a U.S. M. R. R. combine coach.

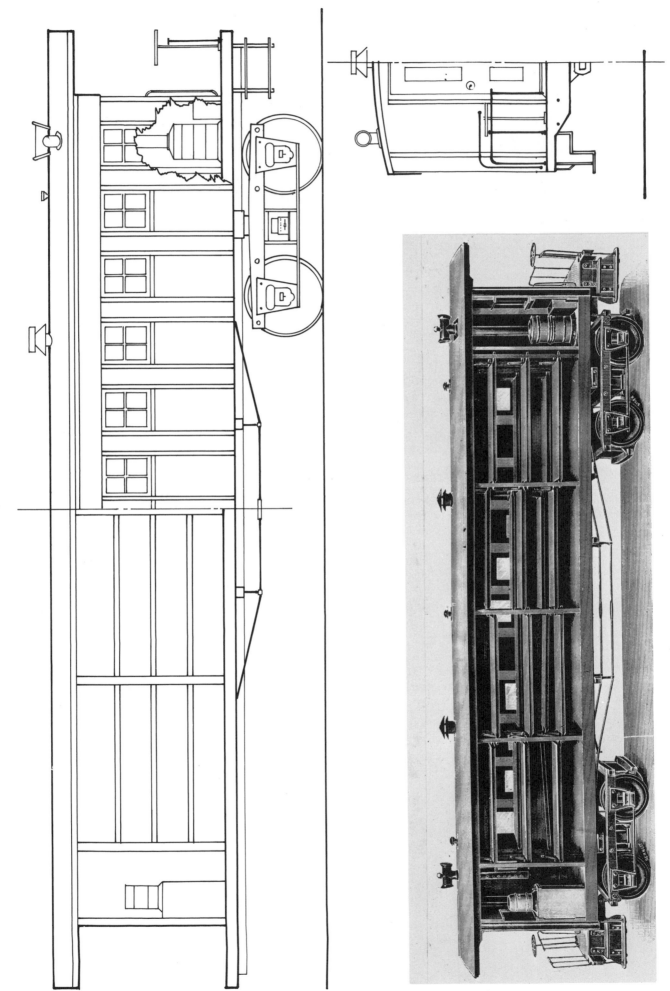

Figure 191. Above: Drawing of hospital car; ¼" scale. *Below:* Cutaway model showing the interior.

Perhaps the most famous passenger car of the 1860s was the private car built for President Abraham Lincoln. The following article by W. H. H. Price, Master Car Builder of the East Tennessee, Virginia & Georgia Railway, which originally appeared in the September 1893 issue of *Locomotive Engineering*, will give the reader an idea of what it was like.

The Private Car Built for President Lincoln, 1863–1865

From time to time since 1866 the writer has noticed in the press and railway journals different articles in regard to the car which was built during the war for the private use of President Lincoln, and, as this important relic (now the property of the Union Pacific Railway) is likely to attract considerable interest among the exhibits at Chicago, he undertakes to state for the benefit of the reading public what he knows of its history. It may be added without impropriety, that there is probably no one now living more conversant with this matter than the writer, as will be shown before he is through.

Soon after the beginning of the war, the old railroad shops at Alexandria, Va. were enlarged by the government for the purpose of building and repairing cars. The work was under the immediate supervision of Mr. B. P. Lamason, superintendent in charge of all car work in Virginia, and the writer was one of his foremen.

Some time during the year 1863 superintendent Lamason either conceived the idea or had received instructions to build a private car for the use of the President. The work was begun in November of that year, and was completed in February, 1865. The car was designed for the general use of the President, and not exclusively for the purpose of conveying him to and from the front, as is generally supposed; neither was the car cased inside with iron as stated by some writers.

As the car was completed but a short time before the assassination of the President, the first trip it ever made was to bear his lifeless remains with those of his son, which had been disinterred from Washington to Springfield, Ill.

After the car was finished, it was photographed by the Government Photographer, from a copy of which, now in the possession of the writer, the accompanying cut is produced.

In design the car was similar to those in use on the Pennsylvania Railroad; it was 42 feet long inside and had a raised roof with circular ends. The inside of the car was upholstered on sides and ends from the seat rail to head lining, and was divided into three compartments, viz., drawing-room, parlor and state room, the latter being the center of the car. The drawing room and parlor were connected by an aisle extending along the wall inside the car, and in the drawing-room end a salon was placed. The upper deck was painted a zinc white, with coats of arms of the different states in the panels.

WASHINGTON.

[SPECIAL DESPATCHES TO THE INQUIRER.]

WASHINGTON, April 21.

Last Sight of the Presidential Remains.

About six o'clock this morning, the members of the Cabinet, the Illinois delegations, the pall-bearers, and several officers of the army with Senators, assembled in the rotunda, and after taking a farewell look at the corpse, it was removed to a hearse by the same sergeants who carried the corpse on Wednesday, and under a guard of honor composed of the companies of Captains Cromee, Bush, Hillebrand and Dillon, of the Twelfth Veteran Reserve Corps, under the command of Lieutenant-Colonel Bell, the remains were taken to the depot, the Cabinet and others following.

The Remains of Little Willie Lincoln.

The remains of little Willie Lincoln, who died in February, 1862, and were placed in a vault at Oak Hill Cemetery, were removed to the depot about the same time, and placed in the same car with the remains of his lamented father. The body was embalmed at the time by Drs. Brown and Alexander, and placed in a metallic burial case, but yesterday the case was placed in a handsome black walnut coffin, silver mounted. The silver plate on the burial case is inscribed, "William Wallace Lincoln, born December 21st, 1850, died February 20th, 1862." The remains of father and son were placed on the car next to the rear one, which was built for the United States Military Railroad originally, for the President and other dignitaries.

The Funeral Train.

It contains a parlor, sitting room and sleeping apartment. Yesterday it was put in mourning by Mr. John Alexander, the windows being hung with black curtains, and the entire furniture robed in black. Along the top, outside, is a row of mourning gathered to black and white rosettes, and another similar row extends around the car, below the window. This car is in charge of Mr. John McNaughton, U. S. M. R. R. A plain stand, covered with black cloth, was placed in the south end of the car on which the remains of the President were placed, and on a like stand, at the opposite end, the remains of little Willie rested. The military, as soon as the remains had passed them, formed in line in front of the building, and a strong guard was placed at all approaches, no person being allowed but officers of the army and navy, the delegations going with the trains, and the passengers for the Philadelphia train leaving at half-past seven o'clock.

At the back of the depot Capt. Camp, of the Soldiers' Rest, posted a guard, and kept the crowd back, a large number of persons having gathered. There were quite a number of officials present as the train was being made ready, among whom were Secretaries Stanton, Usher, Welles, McCulloch and Post Master-General Dennison, Attorney-General Speed, Lieutenant-Gen. Grant, Generals Hunter, Hardee, Barnard, Rucker, Townsend, Ekin, Eaton, Howe, Hall, McCollum, Captain Camp, of Soldiers' Rest, and others of the army. Admiral C. H. Davis, of the Bureau of Navigation, Captain W. R. Taylor and Major Feld of the Marine Corps.

As the time for the departure of the train drew near the parties holding tickets took their places in the train. The station, which, since the death of the President, has worn mourning on the outside, was elaborately draped inside, this morning, the work having been done yesterday, under the direction of Mr. George S. Koontz, the General Agent of the road. Now every window and door frame being draped, and heavy festoons falling from the cornice of the main saloon, and a large flag covered with crape hanging over the door leading to the platform; over the gate to the platform a large arch covered with mourning was sprung, and the railway running the entire length of the platform was covered. The train in which were the remains and those accompanying them was composed of eight cars, six of them being the beautiful double-deckers of the Baltimore and Ohio Road. One, the car from the Military Railroad above described, and the last the one intended for the family and the Congressional Committee, sent here yesterday by the Superintendent of the Philadelphia, Wilmington and Baltimore Road. This car contains a parlor, chamber, dining-room and kitchen, and is elegantly furnished.

The train was put together by Mr. John Collins despatcher of trains, while Mr. Koontz, the General, and Walker the Passenger Agents, saw that the passengers were properly seated. The train was under the immediate charge of Captain J. P. Dukehart, who goes through with the remains to Springfield, as special aid to General McCollum. The engine to go before the train as the pilot was No. 239, of which William Galloway is the Engineer, and James Brown Fireman. It was heavily draped in mourning, all the brass being covered, while in front there were two large flags fringed with mourning, and four smaller ones on the engine. The tender was also heavily draped.

At precisely ten minutes to eight o'clock, after directions had been given by Major-General Meigs and General McCollum, the engine started. Shortly after the pilot engine started, all who were to accompany the remains took their places in the cars, and at eight o'clock the signal was given, when the bell on the engine attached to the train, No. 238, which was dressed as the pilot engine, slowly tolled, the bells on some of the other engines tolling simultaneously, and slowly the train moved from the station, the members of the Cabinet, and others who were on the platform, as well as the crowd gathered in the rear of the depot outside of the line of sentries, standing uncovered until the train passed out of view, when all returned through the station. The engineer in charge of No. 238 was Thomas Beckitt, whose fireman is C. A. Miller, and on the engine was Mr. John R. Smith, Supervisor of Engines of the Baltimore and Ohio Railroad.

Figure 192.   Newspaper story of the Lincoln funeral train, Philadelphia *Inquirer,* April 22, 1865.

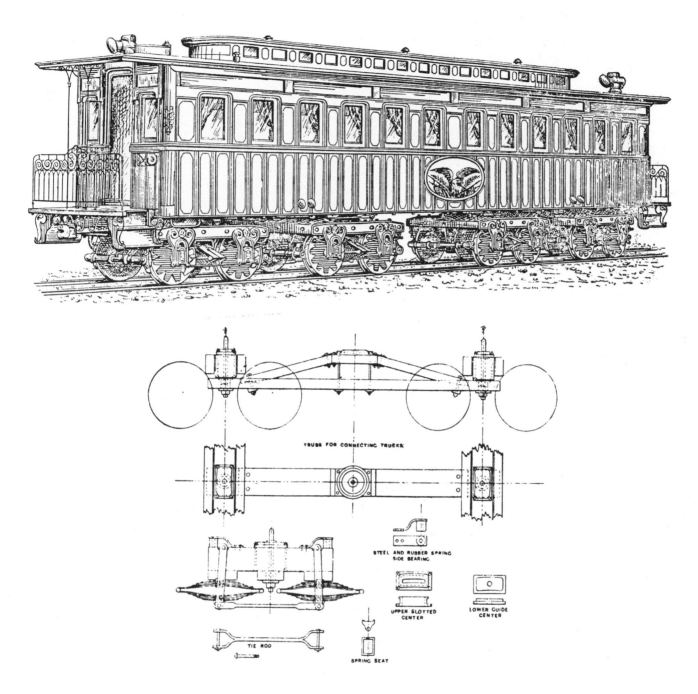

Figure 193.   Above: Drawing of the Lincoln car. *Below:* The four-wheel truck assembly; details.

Figure 194. The Lincoln car and one of the Philadelphia, Wilmington & Baltimore Railroad cars that accompanied it for the family and Congressional committee.

The car was originally planned to run on two trucks, but after being raised, braced and bolted, Mr. Lamason changed his mind and decided to mount it on four trucks, which necessitated changing the bolsters and considerable other work. The body bolsters were Ambrose Ward's patent, and the sides of the car were covered by brass-capped nuts.

Each two pair of trucks was connected by means of a truss, with main center plate in center, and four guide center plates with curved slots, one on each truck. There were eight side bearings made of spring steel and rubber.

The spread of the trucks was 4 feet, 10 inches; wheels 33 inches, cast iron with broad tread. The springs in truck bolsters were hung on old style long hangers, no sand board, but bottom of hangers tied with "U" shaped under roads.

No equalizing bar was used, the elliptic springs being placed on top of the oil boxes. The pedestals were cast iron of a pattern so elaborate as to be difficult to describe, Mr. Lamason having spent weeks in designing them.

The outside of the car was painted a rich chocolate brown, and polished with oil and rotten stone with the bare hand. In the oval center, on side of car, was painted the United States Coat of Arms, and in the center of the panel above the coat of arms, in small gold letters placed in a circle, were the words "United States." Car was ornamented in gold, but neither number nor name except as described.

When the car was returned to Alexandria, it was still draped in black crape, which was removed, carefully boxed and sent to the Treasury Department. The writer had the honor of attending personally to this work, and in spite of orders to the contrary, a small portion of the drapery was secured, a small piece of which he still has in his possession, as well as a block of wood from the catafalque on which rested the body of the dead President.

CHAPTER XI
Freight Cars

THE MANY DIFFERENT TYPES of burden or freight cars in the 1860s is indicated by the Baltimore & Ohio and the Pennsylvania listings that follow. Perhaps the smaller total of the Pennsylvania Railroad's cars was because it was not as old a company and had already started to standardize.

Coal was just beginning to be used as locomotive fuel. A surprising number of B & O iron coal cars carried it for other uses, much of it for city gas plants as well as for industrial and domestic use. *House cars* was the earlier term for boxcars. We can only guess what function other cars fulfilled, using their names as clues. Would a supervisor's car be something that later became the caboose? Would a rigger's car be the forerunner of a crane or wrecking car?

Way cars appears to have been the name for caboose. The first mention of the cabin car, later called the caboose, is found in an 1868 Pennsylvania Railroad report. Note in the way car drawings (Figure 202, etc.) the small raised boxes at diagonally opposite ends of the car roof to hold lanterns, probably the beginning of the use of marker lights. These also appear in old photographs of other cars.

The iron eight-wheel B & O coal cars were unusual in another way than their shape. The eight wheels supporting the car were not in two trucks but in rigid frames, as the drawing and photographs show. Enough lateral play was allowed for the wheels and axles on curves. As the entire car frame totaled only seventeen feet, this was not too much of a problem.

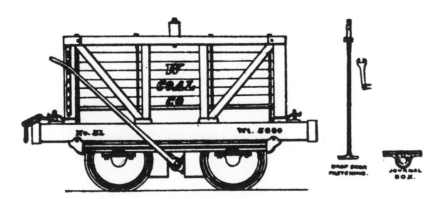

Figure 195a. Old ¼"-scale drawing of a four-wheel coal dinky.

197

Figure 195b. Four-wheel coal cars in an old photograph.

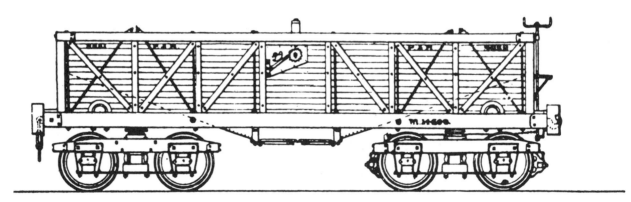

Figure 195c. Drawing of an 1855 Philadelphia & Reading eight-wheel gondola; ¼″ scale.

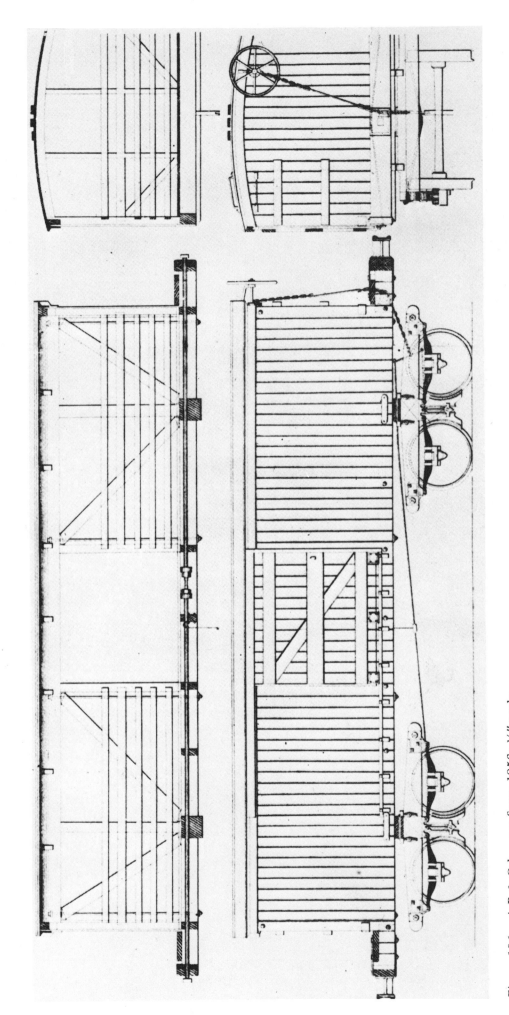

Figure 196. A B & O boxcar from 1856; ¼″ scale.

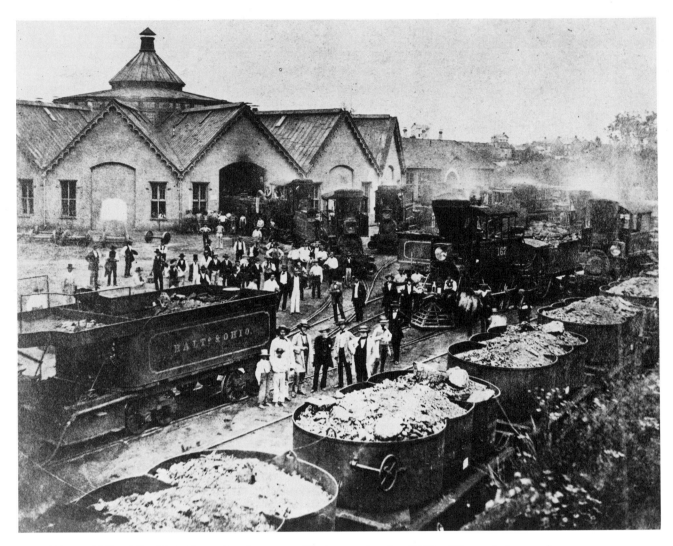

Figure 197. The B & O engine house at Piedmont in the 1860s. Most of the engines are *Camels;* triple hopper iron coal cars are in the foreground.

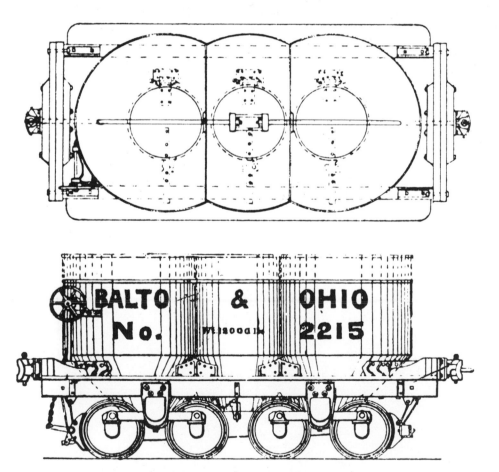

Figure 198. *Above:* A B & O iron coal car of the late 1850s. *Below:* A ¼″-scale plan and elevation of the car. There were no trucks; all four axles were in line, allowing for some lateral play.

Number and Kind of Freight Cars in 1860
(from company reports)

BALTIMORE & OHIO

Eight-wheel house cars	1,135
Eight-wheel gondolas	700
Four-wheel gondola	1
Four-wheel house	5
Eight-wheel barrel	4
Eight-wheel drovers	8
Eight-wheel supervisor's	3
Eight-wheel collector's	1
Eight-wheel cylinder powder	1
Eight-wheel rigger's	5
Eight-wheel house stock	25
Eight-wheel stall stock	10
Eight-wheel open rack, wood	8
Eight-wheel open roof, stock	21
Eight-wheel double deck rack	86
Eight-wheel firewood	17
Eight-wheel stone	52
Eight-wheel lumber trucks	22
Eight-wheel iron coal cars	772
Six-wheel iron coal cars	250
Four-wheel dump	128
Four-wheel stone	14
Four-wheel railroad iron cars	4
Four-wheel broom cars	9
Four-wheel salt car	1
Four-wheel lumber trucks	2
Six-wheel snow plows	16
Four-wheel street plow	1
Eight-wheel scale car	1
Total:	3,302

PENNSYLVANIA

Eight-wheel house cars	1,330
Eight-wheel powder	4
Eight-wheel stock	266
Eight-wheel truck coal and lumber	415
Eight-wheel truck, wood	72
Four-wheel house	116
Four-wheel coal	106
Four-wheel gravel	87
Eight-wheel scale car	1
Total:	2,619

Figure 199. A ¼"-scale model of a U. S. M. R. R. boxcar.

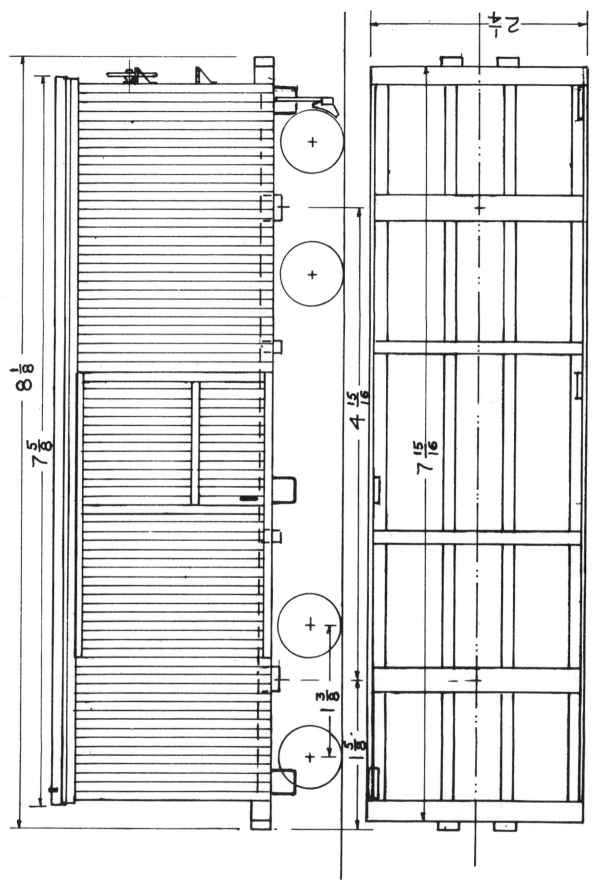

Figure 200. Side elevation and plan, ¼″ scale, of the boxcar.

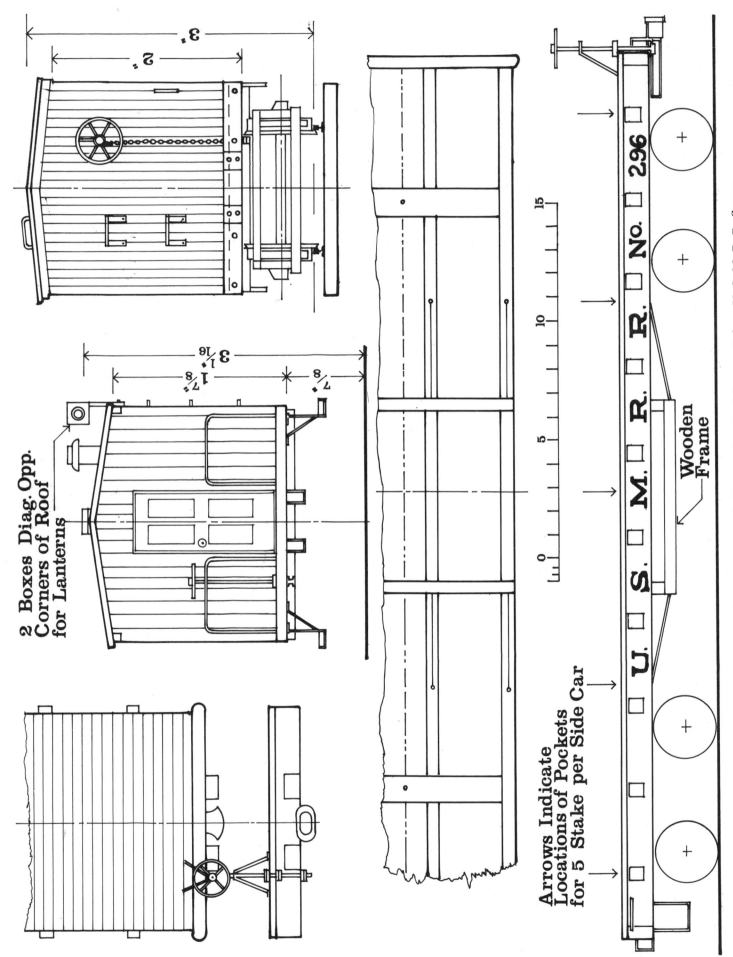

2 Boxes Diag. Opp.
Corners of Roof
for Lanterns

U. S. M. R. R. No. 296

Wooden
Frame

Arrows Indicate
Locations of Pockets
for 5 Stake per Side Car

3'

2'

3 1/16"

1 7/8"

7/8"

0   5   10   15

Figure 201.   Above, right: End of way car. Left: Plan and end of boxcar. Center: End of way car. Below: U. S. M. R. R. flatcar.

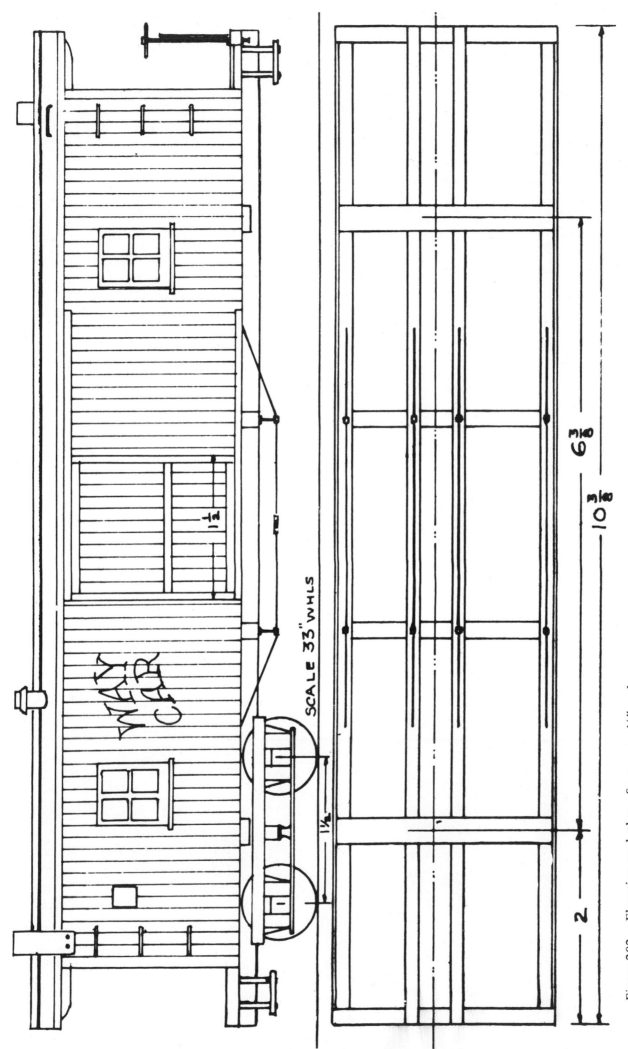

SCALE 33" WHLS

Figure 202. Elevation and plan of way car; ¼" scale.

Figure 203. Model of the way car; ¼″ scale.

Figure 204. *Left:* End of a low side P. R. R. gondola. *Right:* U. S. M. R. R. boxcars at Nashville.

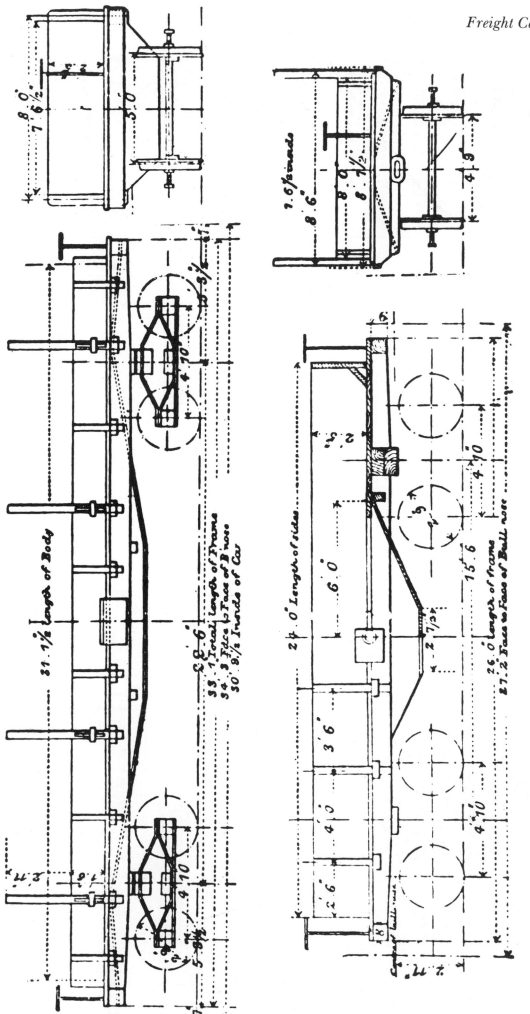

Figure 205. *Above:* P. R. R. coal car. *Below:* P. R. R. gravel car. Both ¼" scale.

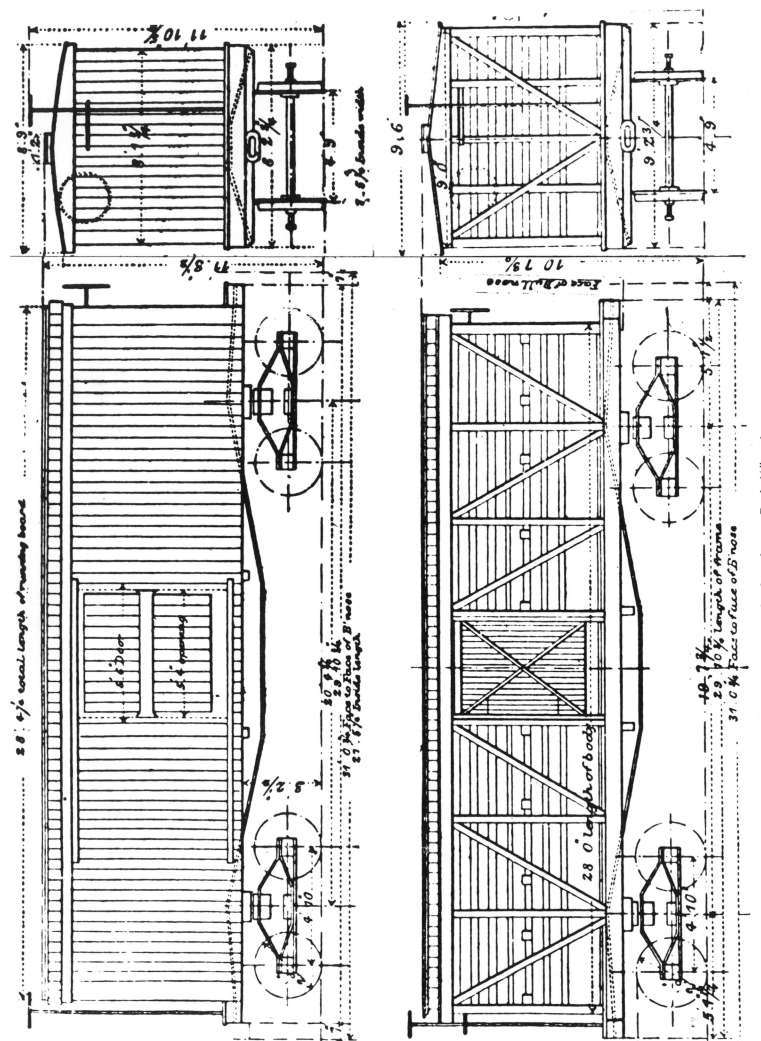

Figure 206. *Above:* P. R. R. standard boxcar. *Below:* P. R. R. standard cattle car. Both ¼" scale.

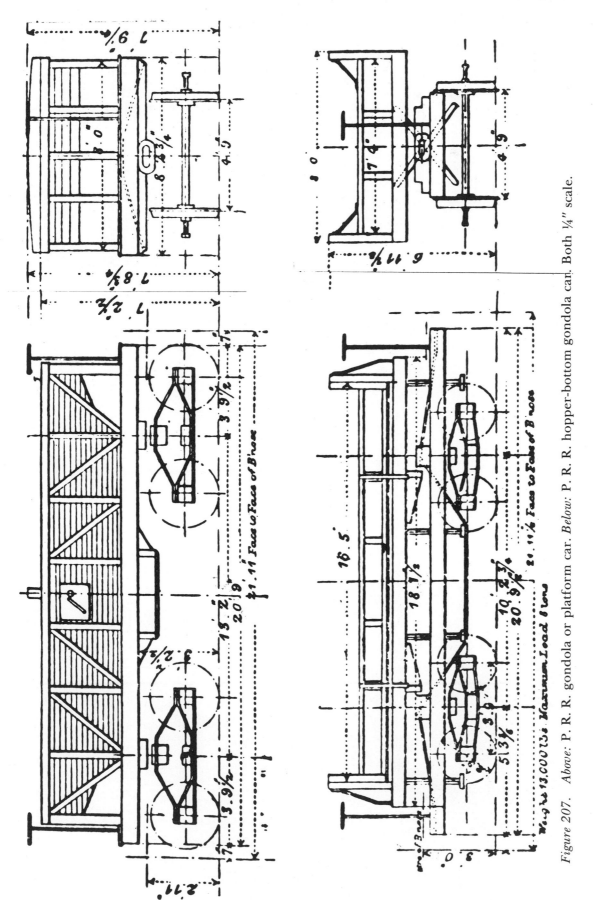

Figure 207. Above: P. R. R. gondola or platform car. *Below:* P. R. R. hopper-bottom gondola car. Both ¼" scale.

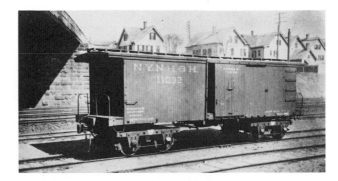

Figure 208. *Left:* An early cattle car. *Right:* An unusual boxcar with platform ends.

Figure 209. Four-wheel dump cars on the B & O at Piedmont, West Virginia, in the 1860s.

Figure 210. A model of a U. S. M. R. R. boxcar and model of the Dictator mortar; ¼″ scale.

CHAPTER XII
Armored Cars

IT WAS LOGICAL and inevitable that the first railroad war would lead to the development of armored gun cars. Records indicate that it was General Robert E. Lee who first suggested building such carriages. On June 5, 1862, he wrote to Col. J. Gorgas, Chief of the Ordnance Department, C.S.A., asking, "Is there a possibility of constructing an iron-plated battery mounting a heavy gun on trucks, the whole covered with iron to move along the York River Railroad? Please see what can be done. See the Navy Department and officers. If a proper one can be got up at once, it would be of immense advantage to me. Have you got any mortars which we could put at some point on the railroad?"

To Capt. George Minor, Chief of Ordnance and Hydrography, also on June 5, Lee wrote:

> The Armstrong gun, if mounted on a field carriage with its supply or projectiles, will be of immense importance to us. Can we not have it in the morning? The smaller gun [the Parrott gun, developed by Robert P. Parrott just before the Civil War] I think we have enough of at present. I am very anxious to have a railroad battery. I wrote to Col. Gorgas on the subject this morning and asked him to get you and Brooke to aid him. Till something better could be accomplished I propose a Dahlgren or Columbiad on a ship's carriage, on a railroad flat and one of your Navy iron aprons adjusted to it to protect gun and men. If I could get it in position by daylight tomorrow I could astonish our neighbors. The enemy cannot get up his heavy guns except by railroad. We must block his progress. Very respectfully and truly, R. E. Lee, General.

On June 21 General Lee wrote in a letter to Secretary of the Navy S. R. Mallory at Richmond that the railroad battery would be ready in the morning and requested an officer and men to man the gun.

On June 14 Col. Gorgas wrote General Lee: "General: The railroad iron-plated battery designed by Lieut. John M. Brooke, C. S. Navy, has been completed. The gun, a rifled and banded 32-pounder of 57 CWT. has been mounted and equipped by Lieut. R. D. Minor, C. S. Navy, and with 200 rounds of ammunition, including 15″ solid bolt shot, is now ready to be transferred to the Army. I have the honor to be . . . George Minor, Commander in Charge."

General Joseph L. Brent of the Confederate Army in his book *Mobilizable Fortifications*, published in 1865 and reprinted in 1916, says,

It was my fortune to witness perhaps the first fire that was ever delivered in actual combat from an armored railway wagon.

During the American Civil War in 1862, the Confederate authorities prepared in Richmond a railway battery armored with railroad iron and carrying a 32-pounder gun in front of the engine. The iron shield only covered the front of the battery, and was pierced by an embrasure, but the sides and rear were unprotected.

When, in June 1862, Lee made his flank movement against McClellan, one of the Seven Days Battles was delivered on the line of the Richmond and York River Railway at a point called Savage Station.

The iron railway battery was sent out on this road from Richmond, and Maj. Gen. MacGruder, commanding the Confederates at Savage Station, ordered this battery to advance and fire on the enemy.

It moved, propelled by steam, down the track, and passed into a deep cut, and from this cut opened with its 32-pound gun, and burst its shell beyond the first line of the Federals, and over the heads of their reserves, forcing them to shift their position.

About the same time skirmishers of the opposing forces became engaged and the lines of battle were deployed, resting on the right side of the railway.

The Union line was a little beyond the cut from which the railway battery fired, and at right angles to it. If the battery had advanced it would have completely enfiladed the Union line at short range, and must have broken it; but owing to the fact that the sides and rear of the battery were open and exposed to the fire of the skirmishers, and to the further fact that the field of fire of the gun was limited by its embrasure, the battery could not advance; and as the skirmish fire approached, it withdrew. If guns had been mounted 'en barbette' and the gunners and machinery protected by bullet-proof armor, and if there had been half a dozen such batteries, they could easily have broken the Federal line of battle, and have cut off their reserves, large numbers of which were stationed on the left of the track.

Figure 211.   A ¼"-scale model of the first armored car suggested by General Robert E. Lee, who on June 5, 1862, suggested in letters to Colonel J. Gorgas, Chief of Ordnance, and Captain George Minor, "a heavy gun on trucks, the whole covered with iron"

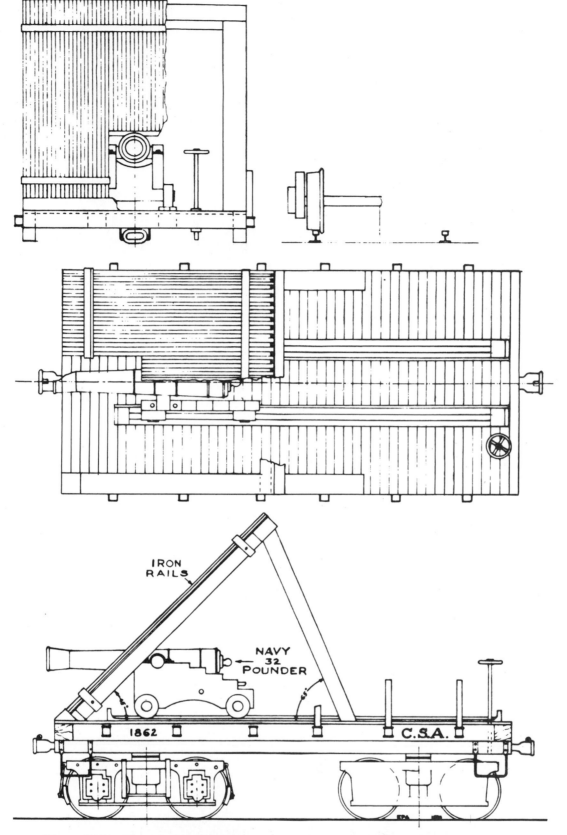

Figure 212. Elevations and plan in ¼" scale of the Confederate gun car.

The drawing of the Confederate gun car (Figure 212) was based on two early sketches from different sources. One designates the shield as having "iron plate" covering. The other's wording is "railway iron," which ordinarily means railroad rails. As the latter was a bit more detailed and as "the railroad iron-plated battery" is mentioned in one of the foregoing letters, Figure 212 was developed from it and the model followed in turn.

Figure 213. Probably the most accurate sketch of an armored car, by William C. Russell. This was evidently used on the Philadelphia, Wilmington & Baltimore Railroad between Baltimore and Havre de Grace in the early days of the war after some bridge burning and skirmishes (see chapter 1).

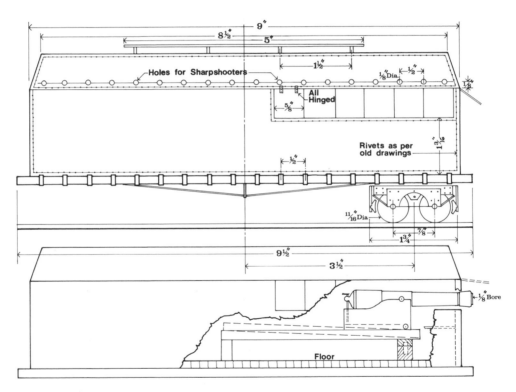

Figure 214. Elevation and vertical section of the foregoing armored car; ⅛″ scale.

Figure 215. A ¼″-scale model of the armored car.

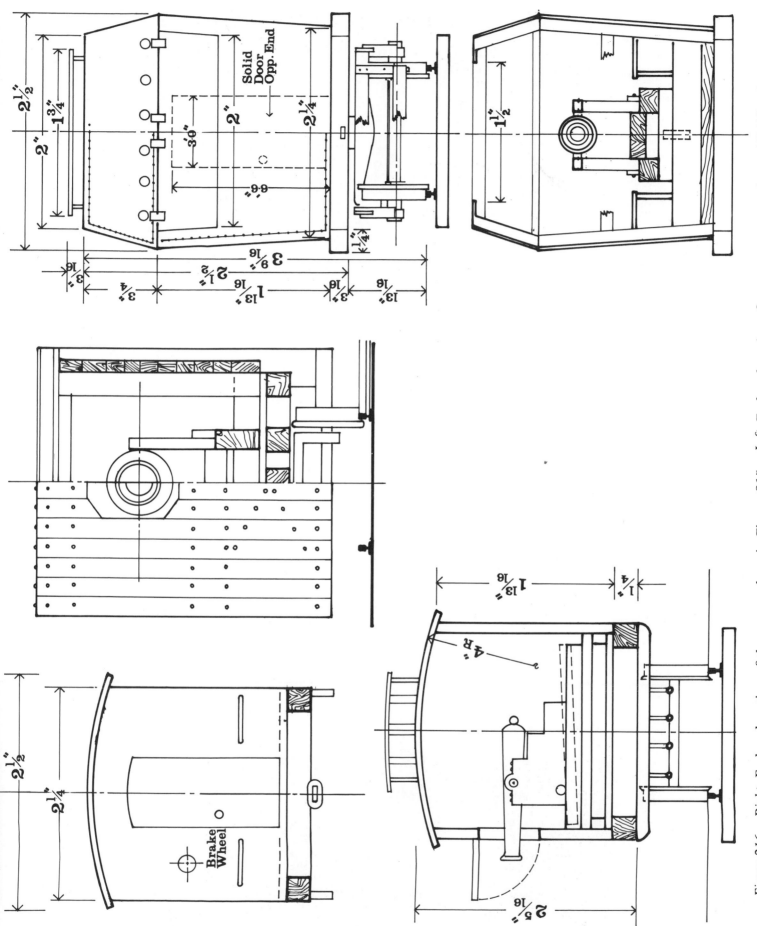

Figure 216. *Right:* End and section of the armored car in Figure 215. *Left:* End and section of a two-gun armored car. All ¼" scale.

Figure 217. First train crossing rebuilt Bull Run bridge with two-gun armored car, spring 1863. The guns faced in opposite directions.

A correspondents' sketch (Figure 213) shows a variation of the armored car used to protect workmen repairing bridges on the Philadelphia, Wilmington & Baltimore Railroad. When this road's right-of-way was secure it was probably transferred to others for similar service. The scale drawing and model were based on Figure 213.

Figure 218. Model in ¼" scale of the armored car in Figure 217.

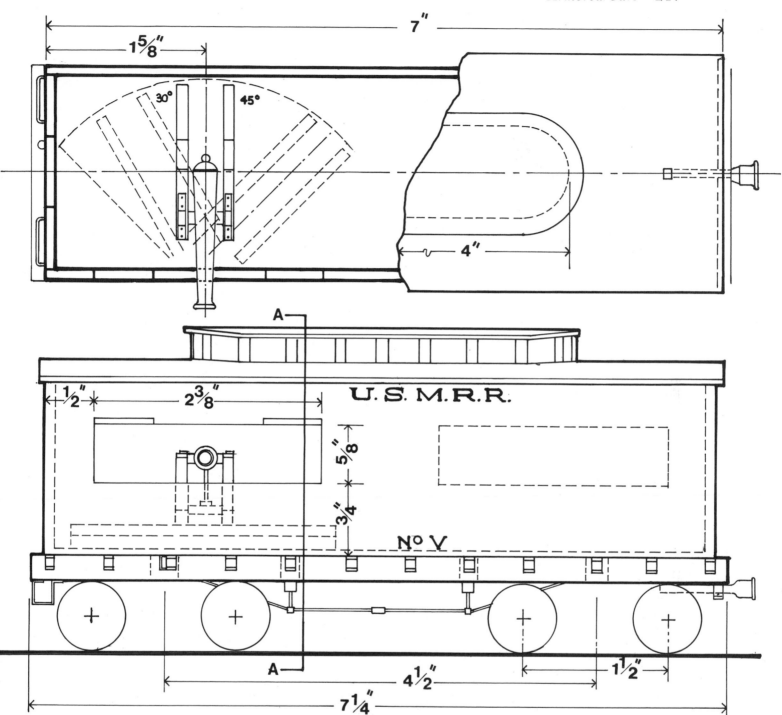

Figure 219. Plan and side elevation of the two-gun car.

In the middle of the train seen in Figure 217 is a little-known armored gun car. Built on a flatcar, as the side stake pockets show, it had two guns facing in opposite directions. The foreshortening and camera angle make it appear almost a four-wheel car at first glance, but drawn in ¼″ scale (Figure 219) it is about the length of a boxcar.

The largest armored gun car was used at the siege of Petersburg in 1864. Mounted on fourteen wheels in three trucks and with some side wall protection for the crew, it had a larger gun than the others. In the absence of exact data for this a Parrott gun appears to

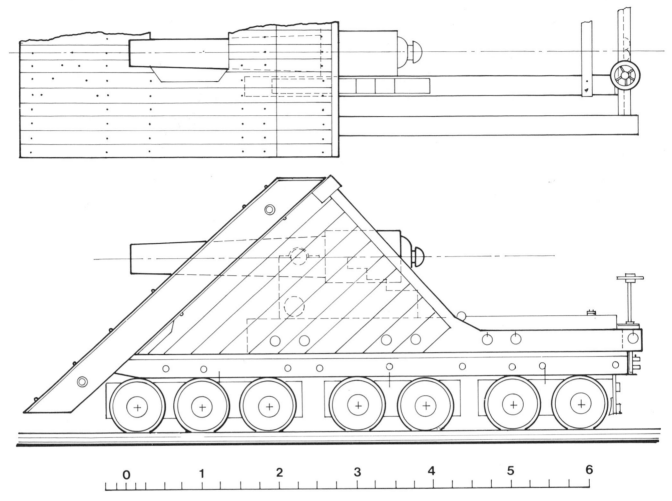

Figure 220.   Plan and side elevation of a fourteen-wheel armored car with a Parrott gun.

have the right proportions and is so depicted in Figure 220. The ring bolts on the lower part of the sides were for ropes by which soldiers could move this weapon without the Confederates being able to locate its position by the sound of a locomotive's exhaust, or so a description states.

Figure 221. Rear view of the fourteen-wheel gun car.

Figure 222. Rear view of a ¼″-scale model.

Figure 223. Side view of the model.

Figure 224. Front view of the model gun car, U. S. M. R. R. boxcar and Dictator mortar.

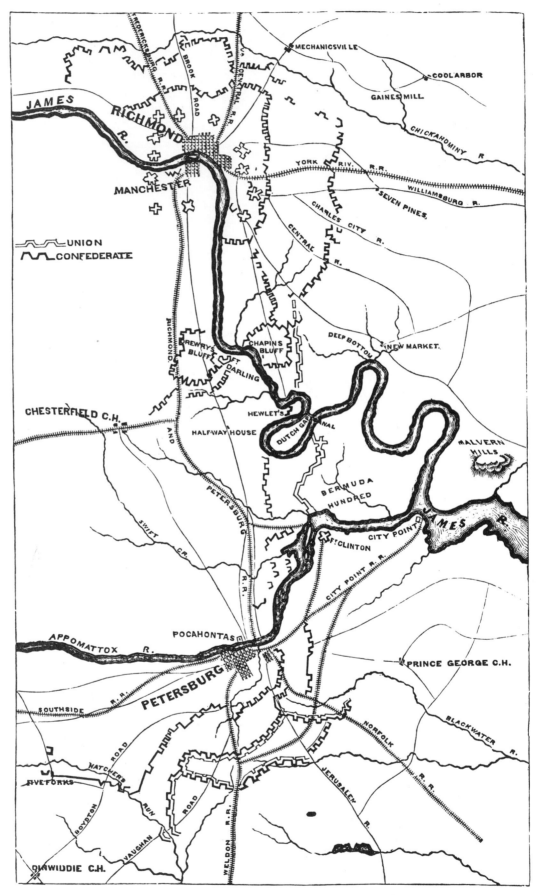

Figure 225. Map of the James River area from Richmond to Petersburg and City Point.

CHAPTER XIII
Military Supply Bases & Camps

THE FIRST GROUP OF PHOTOGRAPHS in this chapter is of City Point, the largest supply base in eastern Virginia, from June 18, 1864, to April 1865. It was located at the junction of the James and Appomattox rivers, where the depth was ample for large ships. Its proximity to Petersburg (six miles) and Richmond (fifteen miles) made it the

Figure 226. An early scene at City Point. The engine *President* is moving fill for additional tracks, to the left.

Figure 227.   The engine house and new track being worked on.

perfect location for dispatching everything needed to the armies of General Grant.

As the photographs show, the base was continually being expanded to handle the increasing amount of stores arriving by ship. Its rail facilities included additional trackage, an engine house, and a turntable.

Other stores and equipment were stockpiled at other less important points, such as Stoneman's Station and Yorktown (Figures 238 and 240).

An idea for a model supply base is shown in Figure 239. It could be varied in size to fit different spaces or be built as an exhibition unit.

Figures 226 through 237 were taken at City Point, Virginia, in 1864. The photographs show the changes in the facilities as they were expanded.

Figure 228. Two views showing the engine house. *Above:* The track between the buildings leads to the turntable.

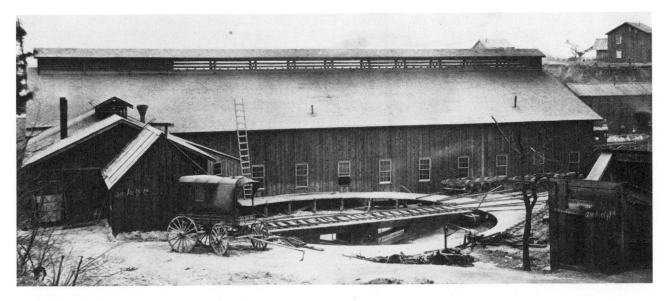

Figure 229. The turntable beside the engine house.

Figure 230. An early wharf being built.

Figure 231. Buildings, probably warehouses, are added.

Figure 232. Trackage on new fill and more construction.

Figure 233. A new temporary trestle and more structures.

Figure 234. Additional filled-in area and trackage and another warehouse.

Figure 235. The scene of reconstruction after the explosion set off by a Confederate agent on August 9, 1864.

Figure 236. A busy scene at City Point, evidently before new warehouses were built.

Figure 237. Soldiers' tents at another area at City Point.

Figure 238.   The Yorktown Military Supply Depot.

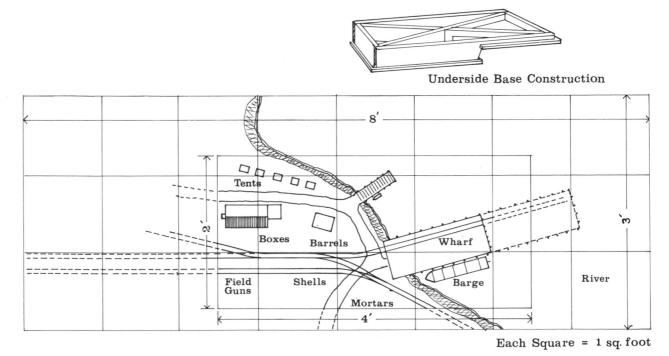

Underside Base Construction

Tents

Boxes   Barrels

Wharf

Field
Guns   Shells

Barge

River

Mortars

Each Square = 1 sq. foot

Figure 239.   A tentative or suggested plan for a small supply base model on a river.

Figure 240.   Another view of Stoneman's.

Figure 241. *Above:* Artillery practice carrying a large shell. *Below:* Caisson and horses after a battle.

CHAPTER XIV
Ordnance

THIS SUBJECT can be only briefly touched on, as the many types of guns, howitzers, and mortars together with their necessary equipment, would require a book in itself. The illustrations that follow are an attempt to show some of the artillery most frequently seen or associated with the Civil War.

Seldom pictured is the equipment that accompanies a field piece, such as a twelve-pounder, before it is set up: the horses, limber, caisson, and more that is usually out of sight to the rear. Figure 1 in Chapter I shows two field guns, about as many as might be used in a model scene, guarding the B & O bridge at Relay. For complete information on this subject the *Artillerist's Manual* (see Bibliography) is recommended.

At the siege of Petersburg in 1864, besides the fourteen-wheel armored gun car (Chapter VII), the mortar *Dictator* or *Petersburg Express* (Figures 244, 246) was in action from July 9 to July 31. Its nine-man crew fired 45 rounds of spherical balls each weighing 220 lbs., with a 20-lb. charge of powder. The 13″ bore mortar weighed 17,000 lbs. Although originally carried on a small two-truck flatcar pushed by a locomotive, its platform was later enlarged, as the illustrations show.

Figure 242a.   A gun crew in action.

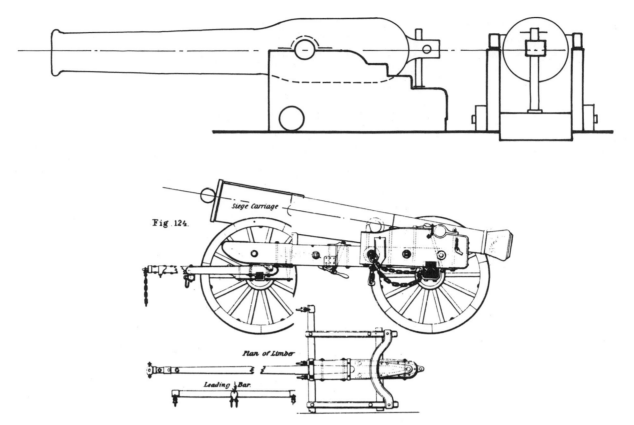

Figure 242b. *Above:* Sketch of a Dahlgren gun; ¼″ scale. *Below:* Drawing of a siege gun carriage; ¼″ scale.

Figure 243. Models, ¼″ scale. *Center, top:* A Dahlgren gun. *Below, left and right:* Parrott guns. *Center, below:* Field gun.

Figure 244. The mortar Dictator or Petersburg Express at the siege of Petersburg.

Figure 245. The Dictator on a larger platform.

Figure 246. A ¼″-scale model of the Dictator with its crew.

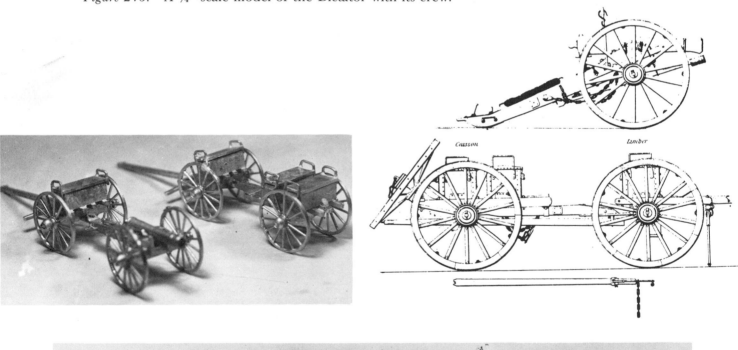

Figure 247. Above: ¼″-scale models and ¼″-scale drawings of a field gun, limber, and caisson. *Below:* Draft horse models for the above.

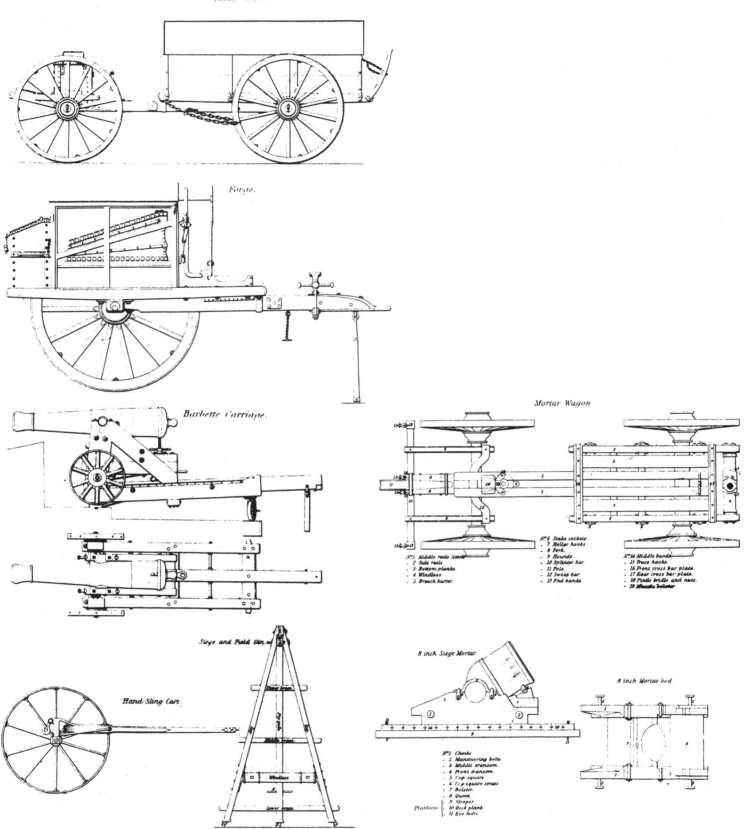

Figure 248. Drawing, ¼″ scale, of battery wagon, a forge wagon, Barbette carriage, mortar wagon, small siege mortar, and embrasure for siege gun.

CHAPTER XV
Alexandria

T HE RAILROAD FACILITIES at Alexandria are particularly interesting because of their importance generally and because of the number of valuable photographs made of equipment there. Occupying the shops of the Orange and Alexandria Railroad, which the U.S. Military Railroad took over, it was a base for supplies for the army and repairs of rolling equipment.

A palisade or stockade was erected surrounding all the railroad facilities, and it may be seen in various photographs in this chapter. The purpose was to provide some protection in case of Confederate cavalry raids.

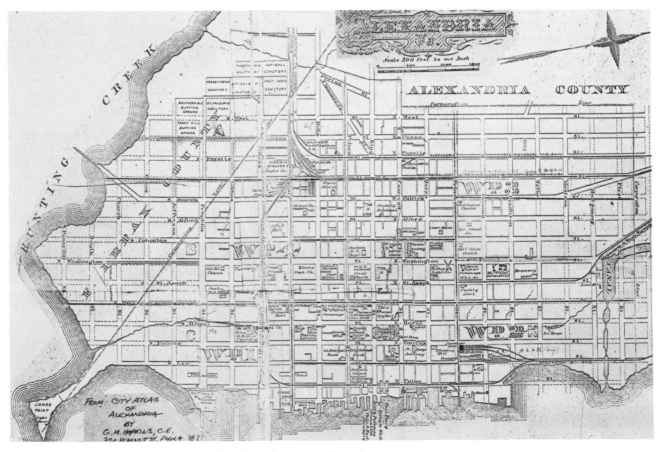

Figure 249.   Map of Alexandria locating its railroads.

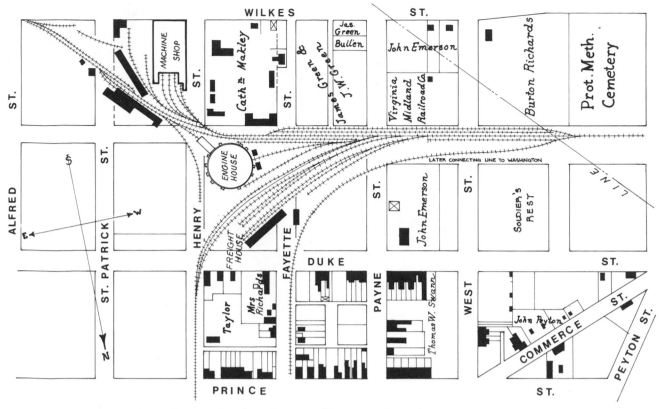

Figure 250. Enlarged map showing the roundhouse and trackage.

The highest point in Alexandria was the cupola on top of the roundhouse, which can be seen in several photographs; later ones show a small platform atop this, from which more pictures were taken.

Many locomotives arrived here in the city, early in the war, from a number of railroads and later from various manufacturers. Necessary repairs were made to rolling equipment in the shops, and cars were also built here, the last one probably being the Lincoln car (Figures 255 and 259).

Figure 251. The *J. H. Devereaux* in front of the Alexandria roundhouse. It was built by the New Jersey Locomotive and Machine Co. of Paterson in 1863. View is looking east–northeast.

Figure 252. The engine house, looking east. The structure to the left is a rectangular water tank. (See chapter 3, Figure 46.)

Figure 253. View north from the roundhouse cupola. Hospital cars in the foreground.

Figure 254. Looking southeast from the roundhouse toward the machine shop.

Figure 255. The car shop from the roundhouse.

Figure 256. A northwest view of the roundhouse. The rear of the tender behind the telegraph pole is lettered *Humming Bird.*

Figure 257. Looking west from the cupola of the roundhouse. Note that all the tracks converge into a single one (Orange & Alexandria Railroad).

Figure 258. The locomotive *General Haupt.*

Figure 259. The car built for President Lincoln in front of the car shop. Never used by him, it carried his body in the funeral train.

Figure 260. The engine *W. H. Whiton,* built by Mason in 1862, with the President's car.

Figure 261. The Lincoln car shortly before it was burned in Minneapolis March 15, 1911.

CHAPTER XVI
Atlanta

FIRST CALLED TERMINUS when the Western & Atlantic Railroad's southern end was located by Chief Engineer Stephen H. Long in 1837, later called Marthasville, Atlanta became an important rail center. Besides the Western & Atlantic, the Georgia Railroad and the Macon & Western connected there.

On April 12, 1862, at Big Shanty, a few miles north of Atlanta, the locomotive *General* and a train of three boxcars were seized by James Andrews and a group of twenty-one men, and headed north. They were shortly thereafter pursued by Conductor (Capt.) W. A. Fuller with the engine *Texas*. This became known as "The Great Locomotive Chase" or "The Andrews Raid." (See Chapter I). Some of the scenes and stations north towards Chattanooga are pictured in Chapter II.

Figure 262. A lithograph from the 1850s showing the train shed (*left*) and the station (*right*).

243

Figure 263. View of the city, July 27, 1864.

Figure 264. The train shed in 1861. (Painting by Wilbur Kurtz.)

Figure 265. Union troops, some on boxcar roofs, preparing to leave. A corner of the station appears at right.

Figure 266. The train shed. The station is to the right opposite the boxcars.

Figure 267. The station appears at left and the train shed, reversed from Figure 266, at right.

Figure 268. The Western & Atlantic Railroad engineering office built in 1842, as painted by Wilbur Kurtz. It was on the north side of what was later Wall Street between Pryor and Central avenues.

Figure 269. The Western & Atlantic roundhouse in 1864. For proportions, the small building in the foreground was sixteen feet square.

Figure 270. Locomotives after the war using the turntable of the destroyed roundhouse. An Atlanta & West Point engine is in the foreground.

CHAPTER XVII
Scenes Worth Modeling

A<small>N INFINITE NUMBER OF SCENES</small> connected with the railroads of the Civil War period have been captured by photographers and war correspondents. To supplement those already presented in this book, a few more are reproduced here to suggest other scenes worth modeling. If a few are not actually in the geographic theater of war, they are of that period and are related scenes.

For example, barges from northern canals brought supplies to bases on the James River, such as City Point, and to Whitehouse landing on the Pamunkey, from which they were transported by rail. Figures 272 and 274 in this chapter and Figure 239 in Chapter XIII pertain.

The last photograph in this section (Figure 280) provides an interesting idea for a small scale setting utilizing an observation balloon. Although not specifically a railroad-oriented subject, the balloon might form part of a background for a railroad scene.

To show how something historical can be created in connection with a model railroad, in addition to operating trains, has been one of the prime objectives of this book. I hope I have succeeded, for the possibilities are endless and fascinating for the hobbyist.

Figure 271. Boxcars and wheels unloaded at Manchester, Virginia.

247

Figure 272.   Barges at Whitehouse Landing on the Pamunkey.

Figure 273a.   Destruction at Fredericksburg.

Figure 273b. *Left:* More destruction at Fredericksburg. *Right:* Culpeper Courthouse.

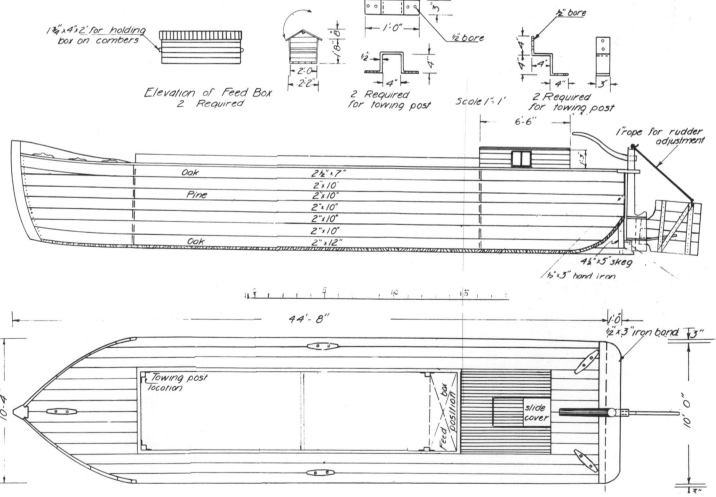

Figure 274. Drawing for a typical barge. Smaller than ¼" scale.

Figure 275.   Station, planked-over track, stub switch, at Marysville, Pennsylvania.

Figure 276.   Fuel station (the building is a water tank) and an early section car at Susquehanna, Pennsylvania. P. R. R.

Figure 277. Canal locks at Jacks Narrows, Pennsylvania, 1860s.

Figure 278. Planked-over track platform at Lewistown, Pennsylvania. P. R. R. Note the large wood rick at right.

Figure 279. Thompsontown, Pennsylvania. Wood rick at right. P. R. R.

Figure 280. Filling an observation balloon. Professor Lowe's *Intrepid,* used to reconnoiter the battle of Fair Oaks, 1862.

Bibliography

AHRONS, E. I. *The British Steam Locomotive 1825-1925*. London: The Locomotive Publishing Co., Ltd., 1925.

Baltimore & Ohio R. R., 32nd through 36th Annual Reports, 1858-1862. Baltimore, Md.

BATES, DAVID HOMER. *Lincoln in the Telegraph Office*. New York: The Century Co., 1907.

BELL, J. SNOWDEN. *The Early Motive Power of the B. & O.* New York: Angus Sinclair, 1912.

BLACK, ROBERT C. *Railroads of the Confederacy*. Chapel Hill: University of North Carolina Press, 1952.

BOWEN, ELI. *Rambles in the Path of the Steam Horse* [early B. & O.]. Philadelphia: Wm. Bromwell & Wm. White Smith, 1855.

COOPER, THEODORE. *American Railroad Bridges*. New York: Engineering News Publ. Co., 1889.

FORNEY, M. N. *Locomotive Building in America* [Rogers Loco. Works]. New York: Wm. S. Gottsberger, 1886.

GIBBON, JOHN. *The Artillerist's Manual* [orig. New York, 1860]. Glendale, N.Y.: Benchmark Publ. Co., 1970.

HUNGERFORD, EDWARD. *The Story of the Baltimore & Ohio Railroad*, 1827-1927. New York: G. P. Putnam & Sons, 1928.

JOHNSON, ANGUS JAMES. *Virginia Railroads in the Civil War*. Chapel Hill: University of North Carolina Press, 1961.

KAMM, SAMUEL RICHEY. *The Civil War Career of Thomas A. Scott*. Philadelphia: University of Pennsylvania, 1940.

LANIER, ROBERT E., ED. *The Photographic History of the Civil War*. 10 vols. New York: Review of Reviews Co., 1911.

LOSSING, BENSON J. *The Civil War Pictorial History*. 3 vols. Philadelphia: George W. Childs, 1868.

MEREDITH, ROY. *Mr. Lincoln's Camera Man, Mathew B. Brady.* New York: Charles Scribner's Sons, 1946.

POLLARD, EDWARD A. *The First Year of the War.* Richmond: West & Johnston, 1862.

Railway & Locomotive Historical Society, various bulletins, esp. 59, 104, 110. Boston, Mass.

STARR, JOHN W., JR. *Lincoln and the Railroads.* New York: Dodd Mead & Co., 1927.

TURNER, GEORGE EDGAR. *Victory Roade the Rails.* Indianapolis and New York: The Bobbs Merrill Co., 1953.

VAN BENTHUYSEN, C. *Maps, Bridges, Profiles, etc.* Report of the Board of Railroad Commissioners, Albany, N.Y.: 1857.

VOSE, GEORGE T. *Manual for Railroad Engineers.* Boston: Lee & Shepard, 1883.

WHITE, JOHN T., JR. *American Locomotives.* Baltimore: The Johns Hopkins Press, 1968.

WILSON, WILLIAM BENDER. *History of the Pennsylvania Railroad.* 2 vols. Philadelphia: Henry T. Coates & Co., 1899.

Sources for Model Components

NORTHEASTERN MODELS, INC., Box 425, Methuen, Massachusetts 01844.
   Basswood.

HOLGATE & REYNOLDS, 601 Davis Street, Evanston, Illinois 60201.
   Plastic sheets, brick, stone, roofing.

E. P. ALEXANDER, Box 333, Yardley, Pennsylvania 19067.
   Locomotives, car components, figures, guns, etc.

KEMTRON CORP., P. O. Box 23068, Los Angeles, California 90023.
   Car components.

GRANDT LINE, 2709 Las Aromas, Oakland, California 94611.
   Building components.

WALTHERS, INC., 4050 North 34th Street, Milwaukee, Wisconsin 53218.
   Car building parts.

U.S. HOBBIES, P.O. Box 12221, Fresno, California 93777.
   Car building parts.

Picture Index